The Mental
and Emotional Life of Teenagers

John J. Mitchell

Detselig Enterprises Ltd.
Calgary, Alberta, Canada

The Mental and Emotional Life of Teenagers

Canadian Cataloguing in Publication Data
Mitchell, John J., 1941-
  The mental and emotional life of teenagers

  Includes bibliographic references and index.
  ISBN 1-55059-211-4

  1. Adolescent psychology. I. Title.
BF724.M562 2001   155.5   C00-911232-4

Detselig Enterprises Ltd.
210, 1220 Kensington Road NW
Calgary, Alberta, Canada T2N 3P5

Phone: (403) 283-0900; Fax (403) 283-6947
email: temeron@telusplanet.net
website: www.temerondetselig.com

We acknowledge the financial support of the Government of Canada through the Book Publishing Industry Development Program (BPIDP) for our publishing activities.

Printed in Canada   SAN 115-0324   ISBN 1-55059-211-4

Contents

This book is dedicated to Mary Jane Mitchell, who, in her twilight years, continues to nurture and guide her seven children.

Preamble

This book investigates the emotional and mental life of teens. Its findings, I fear, will prove painful to those who are steeped in the romantic theories of adolescence which blindly glorify all things youthful, but, on the other hand, encouraging to those willing to see teenagers as they are and not as you might hopefully imagine them to be.

Of profound significance to those of us who nurture and educate the young is their vast potential which does not always express itself in an upward direction. All teens hold not only the potential to progress, but also to regress, not only to march forward, but also to backslide, not only to rise upward but also to spiral downward. Many parents and teachers don't seem to comprehend this developmental truism; they are so indoctrinated with the glory of "upward and outward" that they seem almost blind to the adolescent's potential for life diminishing, regressive choices. One of the cherished illusions held by these romantics is that youth possess some built-in beacon which wisely directs them, but this simply is not the way it is. Youth have inner whisperings, to be sure, but no clarion call, no unfailing instincts, no persistently right urges to chart their direction.

Neither the potential, nor the dignity, of youth blossom on their own; indeed, on their own, they are very likely to wither and weaken. To attain full measure, the potential of youth must be nurtured by the encouragement, the leadership, and the wisdom of caring, competent adults. This is perhaps the foremost lesson we have learned from the scientific study of adolescence – teens do not grow straight and strong without great assistance from their elders.

Human potential is capable of a wide variety of different expressions; it doesn't come with any guarantees. For adolescents and their loved ones this holds profound practical consequences. It means that the adolescent potential for clear thinking may express itself as clear thinking, or as murky, beclouded thinking; that the adolescent potential for intimacy and love may express itself as intimacy and love, or as distant indifference; that the adolescent potential for altruism and community may express itself as altruism and community, or as selfish isolationism. In other words, potential has many destinations, some far better than others.

Youth require a good deal of help to actualize their potential with dignity and humanity. The extent we, as a society, are providing this necessary help to our young is one of the underlying themes in the upcoming chapters.

In this book we will examine the mental and emotional forces which encourage adolescents to actualize their potential in ways beneficial to their own individual growth and to the betterment of their society. We will also consider those forces which encourage a downward spiral in their aptitude and attitude – forces which degrade the quality of teen life and which diminish the society which nurtures them.

Hopefully, our investigation will move us a step closer to a fair and honest understanding of the mental and emotional life of teenagers.

John J. Mitchell
Okanagan University College
January, 2001

Section One

Intelligence and Counter Intelligence

One

The Higher Levels of Adolescent Thought

All rising to a great place is by a winding stair. (Francis Bacon)

The intellectual skills of teen-agers guided their thought and behavior long before they first became the object of scientific investigation in the early 1900s. Our investigation will not resolve the mysteries surrounding adolescent intelligence, but it will attempt to define them with more realism than has been customary in adolescent psychology during the past four or five decades.

Here I want to tell something of the story about the incredible potential which graces adolescent intelligence – the higher reaches of adolescent thought. This story comes at a time in our understanding when we adults (and scholars) are quite confused about what the adolescent thinker can and cannot do, a confusion spiced by the adolescent's ability to comprehend calculus but not speed limits, Malthusian population theory but not birth control, the authority of the State but not the parent.

In this chapter the focus is on the higher reaches of adolescent intelligence, and only its higher reaches. (The lower reaches of adolescent thought, every bit as numerous and challenging, are given their coverage in upcoming chapters.)

"Higher reaches" and "lower reaches" are labels I use to get at the perplexing duality of intelligence. The thought process which guides adolescent judgment, decision-making, and behavior is neither bright nor dull, it is both; neither rational nor irrational, it is both; neither fair nor prejudiced, it is both. To complicate things even further, adolescents themselves don't always know when the bright or dull rays of intelligence direct their mental activity.

How do we assess a mental force which operates at such contrasting levels of proficiency, a force which can both enliven and deaden intellectual vitality? You set forth both and hope one illuminates the other.[1]

•   •   •

Adolescent thinking is usually compared with either the thinking of adults or with the thinking of children. Those who compare adolescents with children conclude that adolescents are exceptionally bright, while those who compare them with adults usually conclude that adolescents have a considerable distance yet to travel. We will begin our investigation with a look at how adolescent thinking compares with that of children.

The thinking of adolescents improves over the thinking of children in at least three ways. First, adolescents are better at seeing the *possible* because their mind is not confined to mere variations of known reality. Second, adolescents are better at devising ways to test what they don't know, to verify unverified hypotheses. Third, they are better at concept manipulation. These three points, significant as they are, do not exhaust the ways adolescent thought soars beyond that of children. So the first thing to keep in mind is that, intellectually, adolescents are not merely "bigger and better" children. They possess intellectual tools which allow them to think in ways completely beyond the capacities of children. The gap separating adolescent intelligence from childhood intelligence is far greater than the gap separating adolescent intelligence from adult intelligence.

Since Jean Piaget first began to explore this mental territory in the 1920s, the intellectual advances which take place during adolescence have been known as "formal thought." In this chapter my focus is on what goes into, and what comes out of, formal thought. As the chapter title suggests, this is a period when intellectual power increases by leaps and bounds over childhood thought. In later chapters I will try to explain why adolescents sometimes use this intellectual power with flare and vitality and why, on other occasions, they use it frivolously, even stupidly, and why, on still other occasions, they don't seem to use it at all. For now, however, our concern is with the higher levels of adolescent intelligence and the mental capacities it brings with it.

Adolescents hold the capacity for advanced and sophisticated thought, and this *capacity*, more than anything else, accounts for our elevated expectations and our increased demands on youth in our culture. Equally important, however, the capacity for advanced thought is not always used; sometimes it remains dormant, and sometimes it is replaced with inferior thinking. This unsettling state of affairs will be investigated later (chapter two through six). For now, our concern is with the mental abilities which produce deep, profound, and analytic thought during the teen years – the higher reaches of adolescent intelligence.

The Power of Adolescent Intelligence

Though the Life Force supplies us with its own purpose, it has no other brains to work with than those it has painfully and imperfectly evolved in our heads. (George Bernard Shaw)

Psychologists have looked at formal thought from many angles over the past several decades. My concern is with the *abilities and competencies* which, taken in their entirety, produce a higher plane of thinking during the adolescent years. This "higher plane of thinking" comes into being with the adolescent's increased capacity for abstraction, increased powers of comprehension, increased capacity for self-analysis, increased facility for analyzing propositions, and increased preoccupation with the future. In the next few pages we will see how these mental abilities give wings to adolescent thought, and, in turn, to adolescent intelligence.

The particulars of formal thought include increased powers of abstraction, increased comprehensiveness, increased skills at self-analysis, advanced capacity for propositional thought, and greater awareness of future time. I will deal with them in that order.

Abstraction. Margaret Donaldson, in her splendid work, *Children's Minds,* which Jerome Bruner claimed was "One of the most powerful . . . books on the development of the child's mind to have appeared in twenty years," made an insightful observation on abstract thinking which is of special value to anyone trying to grasp the differences between "concrete" thinkers (this usually means children) and "formal" thinkers (which usually means adolescents).[2]

> It is when we are dealing with people and things in the context of fairly immediate goals and intentions and familiar patterns of events that we feel most at home. And when we are asked to reason about these things . . . we can often do it well. So long as our thinking is sustained by this kind of human sense, and so long as the conclusion to which the reasoning leads is not in conflict with something which we know or believe or want to believe, we tend to have no difficulty. Thus even pre-school children can frequently reason well about the events in the stories they hear. However, when we move beyond the bounds of human sense there is a dramatic difference. Thinking which does move beyond these bounds, so that it no longer operates within the supportive context of meaningful events, is often called 'formal' or 'abstract.'

Moving beyond the bounds of our immediate human sense to a realm where ideas may have nothing to do with ourselves or our own immediate lives is the challenge of abstract reasoning. And this is the first quality which separates the thinking of teens from the thinking of children – the capacity to *systematically* manipulate and organize the abstract. To think about the remote, the impossible, the unimaginable.

Comprehensiveness. When solving problems children do not usually recognize that an unexplored possibility could be as correct as a more obvious possibility. Adolescent thought, on the other hand, is less susceptible to leaving out critical facts, less prone to errors of omission, and less likely to believe that the right answer has been found when one of the options seems immediately reasonable. In sum, formal thinkers not only consider many possibilities, they *try* to consider all possibilities, this, in turn, allows them to plan in considerable detail what they are going to do, and to interpret whatever they do within the total context. In contrast, children tend to think on a case-by-case basis and to plan less systematically. This leads them to leap to conclusions too quickly, and to believe as true what is only partly true.

Comprehensiveness requires the ability to consider the effects of two, three, even four variables at the same time, a skill known as *combinatorial thinking*. This skill, like so many skills necessary for formal thought, exists only in subdued form during childhood, but blossoms brightly in adolescence.

Without intellectual comprehensiveness, scientific analysis and philosophical reasoning are not possible. Comprehensiveness signals an awareness that any given problem cannot be solved *with certainty* until all of the variables pertaining to it are taken into account. It is the mental attribute of great detectives, methodical scientists, and competent criminals.

The object of its own investigation. To children, a thought is a thought is a thought. Adolescents, however, realize that a thought may be born to rich or poor parentage, and that it can be strongly or weakly constructed, that it can be worthy or worthless. Children possess very few standards by which to judge whether one thought is more valid than another; adolescents, on the other hand, become increasingly adept at employing verifiable standards when seeking the truth.

When we say that thought "becomes the object of its own action," we mean that it can double-check itself, re-trace its own steps to detect mental errors made along the way. Walking back through one's own intellectual journey is one of the most profound breakthroughs in human intelligence. Now the thinker can actually interrupt the thought process to ask: "Am I thinking this through clearly?" "Have I left anything out?" "Have I paid too much attention to one side of the issue at the expense of the other?" After such a re-think the thinker might even say: "Let me go through this one more time." The net effect is that the thinker is no longer at the mercy of the "first presentations" of the thought process, which is to say that the thinker no longer merely accepts mental conclusions "as delivered." The thought process becomes accountable to its own internal audit, hence, more and more ideas are rejected as unfit. This capacity to reject an idea when it lacks coherence represents an advance over the child's intellect which, generally speaking, does not double-check its own conclusions nor evaluate them by a higher standard. The process of self-examination we are discussing here is what Albert Camus had in mind when he claimed that "An intellectual is someone whose mind watches itself." A mind which watches itself is a "formal" mind.

Because the adolescent thought process analyzes and evaluates itself, it transcends the more earthy thought of childhood. This, quite obviously, is no real surprise as no one, to my knowledge, claims that children are loftier thinkers than adolescents. (The issue lurking in the background is how the higher reaches of adolescent thought compare with the higher reaches of adult thought.)

Formal thought does not operate at peak efficiency all of the time; indeed, it appears to not work at all some of the time, and in some individuals it seems to never work. To operate efficiently, formal thought must be beckoned; it is not "natural," emerging spontaneously and without effort. Formal thought is influenced by the discipline and the training of the thinker in whom this potential resides, the same as athletic or artistic potential.

In future chapters we will pay close attention to the forces which prevent adolescents from thinking clearly, from double-checking and cross-referencing their own thoughts. We do this for a simple reason: thinkers who do not double-check their own thought process for errors, omissions or contradictions think, for the most part, as children.

Propositions. A proposition is any statement capable of being believed, doubted, or denied. Propositions can be debated, analyzed and dissected; they are not bound to as-is reality, indeed, the most exciting ones are grounded in as-if speculation. Propositional thought allows one to investigate ideas beyond reality *as realilty is presently understood.* To go back to Piaget: "Reality becomes secondary to possibility."[3]

Propositional reasoning goes beyond everyday experience to investigate things never directly experienced, to quiz remote abstractions, to speculate about the unreal. Propositional reasoning also allows one to reason about false hypotheses and to draw logical conclusions from them. Here, again, Wadsworth helps us.

> If a logical argument is prefixed by the statement "Suppose coal is white," the concrete operational child, when asked to solve the problem, declares that coal is black and that the question cannot be answered. The child with formal operations readily accepts the assumption that coal is white and proceeds to reason about the logic of the argument. *The older child can submit to logical analysis the structure of the argument, independent of the truth or falseness of its content.* (1989, p. 118)

In contrast to the formal thinker, children focus on the perceptible elements of a problem and speculate rarely about possibilities which do not bear directly on the matter at hand. They eagerly wade into a problem with no real strategy, no intellectual "game plan." When they solve a problem correctly, they may not know how they solved it, or when faced with a similar problem, they may not be able to beckon the strategies that only a few minutes before they used so effectively.

Political thought also undergoes a significant transformation during adolescence, precisely because the formal thinker can now investigate theoretical scenarios never before considered, and examine ideological propositions inconceivable to a less mature mind.

Eventually, the mental furniture of concrete thought, so neatly arranged and tightly spaced, gives way to a more expansive reason, and it does so largely because of propositional thought. While first flexings are rather modest, they are the first organized attempt to deal with the complexities of advanced intellectualism; indeed, without propositional thought, philosophy, and political theory (as we know them) are impossible.

Future-oriented. Concrete thinkers are not chained to the present, but neither are they free to take flight from it; their mental centre is "here and now" not "there and then." Formal thinkers, on the other hand, are more liberated from the clock, even the calendar; they glide through light years, infinity, and timelessness in ways that concrete thinkers cannot even begin to contemplate. As Bleiberg expressed it: "In their heads, using only thoughts and words, adolescents can project themselves into the future (the realm of the possible), and in so doing can explore the full range of possibilities inherent in a problem (1994, p. 40).

With formal thought, immediate time is recognized as a flicker of eternal time, clock time is differentiated from experiential time; geological *and* astronomical time take hold. The adolescent's transformation to future-oriented thought is profound for many reasons but perhaps the most important is that thought is inherently narrow when bound to the present.

The adolescent's ability to think about the future infuses new mystery and new possibility into the identity project; indeed, a great share of the adolescent's identity quest is based on anticipation of how the future will unfold. The ambitions, aspirations, and dreams of the identity project, the anticipation of the next decade of life, are given their form and content by the mental attribute of future analysis.

Without future-oriented thought the grand disciplines of theology and cosmology cannot be. Neither can personal identity be meaningfully constructed without an eye trained on the future.[4]

Summing up the Advances of Formal Thought

Decision making has certain basic elements: Stop and think; get information; assess information, including consequences; consider options, or formulate options; try new behavior and get feedback. These are fundamental elements of decision making that contribute to healthy adolescent development. (David Hamburg)

The genius of human intelligence is bound to these mental advances, which sprout during adolescence. Even though these breakthroughs in thinking capacity are developmentally driven, and honor fairly specific chronological time-tables, they do not reach their full force, their full majesty, without teaching, training, and coaching.

In the end we come to see that the advances of formal thought, taken in their totality, dignify human thought by empowering the intellect to:

- Go beyond the real to investigate the ideal;
- Go beyond the physical to investigate the hypothetical;
- Go beyond fragments to investigate wholes;
- Go beyond "what is" to investigate "what if";
- Go beyond the present to investigate the future.

Important Differences Between the Child Thinker and the Adolescent Thinker

Aristotle laid down as an axiom of logic what is now known as "the principle of contradiction." He described it this way: "It is impossible for the same attribute at once to belong and not to belong to the same thing in the same relation." This principle allows us to conclude, among other things, that a thing cannot be itself and its opposite at the same time. I have spent a number of years teaching this principle to teens, and I have found that, despite its obtuse language, it is quite understandable to most of them. Concrete thinkers, on the other hand, wrestle with this axiom, but they never seem to pin it down; it is too elusive and too cumbersome for them. In this example we see an important difference between the concrete and the formal thinker.

One of the challenges facing anyone who investigates the adolescent thought process is doing so without making teens appear, on the one hand, incompetent or trivial, or, on the other hand, masterful and profound.[5] Neither extreme is an accurate portrayal, yet both are correct some of the time. If we were to condense a great amount of research into one brief sentence, it might read like this: the thinking of adolescents is profoundly richer than the thinking of children but less profound than the thinking of adults.

The point to be seized is that the thinking of children is locked into its own primitive mechanics. Children think transductively, which is to say that they infer a particular fact from another particular fact. Usually only an isolated part of a problem is seen. The child, for the most part, deals with only one problem at a time, and will oversimplify complex situations, all of which leads to unsystematic thinking, illogical and inconsistent conclusions. The major disability in children's thinking is their lack of reversibility, the inability to double-check the evidence in the light of conclusions reached.

In practical terms, teens possess certain mental abilities which children do not; mental abilities which allow them to think about the possible as well as the real; to think about implications as well as facts; to think about alternatives as well as givens; to think about hypotheses as well as descriptions; to think about "what if" as well as "what is." In addition to all this, adolescents, especially older ones, are beginning to recognize how difficult it is to be absolutely certain about concepts and abstractions; they recognize the finiteness of human intelligence, and demonstrate a certain humility in the face of what they cannot grasp. In my years as a developmental psychologists, I have never met a twelve-year-old who grasped the meaning behind the following statement by one of the 20th century's great thinkers, Paul Tillich, but, on the other hand, I never met a university student who was not greatly impressed by it. "Knowledge of reality never has the certainty of complete evidence. Every knowledge of reality by the human mind has the character of higher or lower probability." Even the most basic of truths must be processed through the frailties of the human intellect, but to recognize our posture of inadequacy requires considerable mental development.

All in all, the probable, the possible, and the theoretical rival material reality as the object of thought. The thinking of children is bound to what is or what is not; the thinking of teens uncovers hidden treasures of the mental universe incomprehensible to the child's mind.[6]

Final Comments on the Higher Reaches of Adolescent Intelligence

The adolescent who insists upon a critical examination of conventional wisdom is making himself into an adult. (Leon Eisenberg)

The adolescent mind is blessed with a tremendous *potential* for reason, for rationality, for intelligence. Without an appreciation of this potential we cannot embrace the heroic possibilities of youth. Yet, without an honest recognition of how easily this potential is eroded, we are blind to the limitations of youth. There is a considerable distance between adolescent intelligence on its own and adolescent intelligence guided by concerned adults and capable peers. This distance is what Lev Vygotsky called the "zone of proximal development," and it interests us because its focus is the same as ours – how the adolescent thought process is improved and upgraded when exposed to excellent mentorship.

We all agree that at their height, formal thinkers calculate with Newtonian precision and infer with Napoleonic swiftness, but we also all agree that formal thinkers are not always "at their height." Formal thought is an ability teens do not always use, and when they do use it, there is no guarantee that they will use it effectively. Individuals capable of formal reasoning sometimes reason on a formal level, sometimes on a concrete level, sometimes on an affective level, and sometimes not at all. To further complicate things, adolescents may employ formal thought effectively in one area and clumsily in another.

Formal thought, it should be noted, does not work solely in support of reason or intelligence; it serves other masters as well, notably, the needs, cravings and desires of the self. Indeed, in many youth, formal thought actually works more aggressively in the service of emotional needs than anything else. As we shall see in upcoming chapters, some youth use their intellect, not for science or reason, but for protection and promotion. This is not a bad thing, but, as far as intellectual development is concerned, a price is paid for seconding the intellect to narcissistic ends.

In conclusion, adolescents are lifted by formal thought and transported to a higher intellectual plane because of it, but this does not mean that their thoughts (or their lives) are always under its influence. If this were the case you would, at this moment, hold in your hands a much briefer book.[7]

Anecdotes and Supplemental Information.

[1]**The brightness and the dimness of the adolescent thought process**. Before one seeks, one must have a lantern; what is found is determined not merely by one's natural acuity, but also by the luminescence of the lantern. To understand how youth seek, and what they are able to find, we must know something of the lantern which guides them. Hence, we have no choice except to investigate both the brightness which illuminates, and the dimness which darkens, the adolescent thought process.

[2]**Formal operations are similar to, yet differ from, concrete operations**. Here is how B. J. Wadsworth explains it:

Functionally, formal thought and concrete thought are similar. They both employ logical operations. The major difference between the two kinds of thought is the much greater range of application and type of logical operations available to the child with formal thought. Concrete thought is limited to solving tangible concrete problems known in the present. Concrete operational children cannot deal with complex verbal problems involving propositions, hypothetical problems, or the future. The reasoning of concrete operational children is 'content bound' – tied to available experience. To this extent, a concrete operational child is not completely free of past and present perceptions. In contrast, a child with fully developed formal operations can deal with all classes of problems. During this stage the child becomes capable of introspection and is able to think about his or her own thoughts and feelings as if they were objects (1989, p. 116).

[3]**Propositional thought.** According to J. H. Flavell, the renowned Piagetian scholar, *propositional thinking* is the starting point of all advanced intellectualism:

The important entities which the adolescent manipulates in his reasoning are no longer the raw reality data themselves, but assertions or statements – propositions – which "contain" these data. What is really achieved in the 7-11 year period is the organized cognition of concrete objects and events per se (i.e., putting them into classes, seriating them, setting them into correspondence, etc.). The adolescent performs these first order operations, too, but he does something else besides, a necessary something which is precisely what renders his thought formal rather than concrete. He takes the results of these concrete operations, casts them in the form of propositions, and then proceeds to operate further upon them, i.e., make various logical connections between them. (1963, p. 205)

[4]Future analysis. The conflict between teleology and determinism has not attracted our attention thus far, and here I shall only briefly outline its relevance to the adolescent experience. Teleology speaks of being directed toward a definite end, of having an ultimate purpose, especially when these ends and purposes derive from a natural process. Teleology is a belief that natural phenomena are determined not only by mechanical causes but also by an overall design or purpose. Determinism, on the other hand, adheres to the doctrine that everything is entirely determined by a sequence of causes, and, as far as human beings are concerned, that one's choices and actions are not free, but determined by causes independent of one's will. Cosmic purpose need not be invoked to account for the adolescent's preoccupation with the future; it derives from the increased mental abilities of formal thought, and from cultural demands to prepare for occupation, marriage, and family.

[5]Overestimating the abilities of teens. M. J. Quadrel et al. (1993) remind us: "We do adolescents a disservice if we overestimate their decision-making competence (hence, deny them needed protections) or if we underestimate it (hence, deny them possible autonomy)." Much of the confusion in adolescent psychology is grounded in the tendency to sometimes overestimate and, at other times, to underestimate the abilities of teens.

[6]Brain development. What is comprehensible or incomprehensible to the child's mind is directly related to brain development during childhood. Great advances in our knowledge of the human brain have taken place in the past several decades, including what we know about how it grows during childhood.

• Increased lateralization. The process by which one side of the brain takes control in organizing a particular mental process or behavior is known as lateralization. As children mature, one hemisphere attains dominance over the other, which permits greater specialization and increased proficiency of psychological functions. Middle childhood is a time of increased brain lateralization, and it is also a time when more complex thought and more effective coordination of action take place. For example, complex behaviors such as writing with a pencil and playing soccer are executed far more effectively in middle childhood. The skills we associate with mid-childhood owe their emergence, in great measure, to increased brain lateralization.

• Brain size and activity. The brain increases in size but also changes its patterns of electrical activity during middle childhood. Between ages five and seven the rate of growth in the surface area of the frontal lobes increases rather sharply. The myelination of the cortex nears completion. The brain wave activity of preschoolers displays more theta activity, which typifies adult sleep patterns; between five and seven years an increase in alpha activity occurs, which is characteristic of engaged attention in the adult. As middle childhood advances, alpha activity increases.

• Brain complexity. By middle childhood the brain has achieved a structural and neurological complexity almost equal to that of adults. The frontal lobes coordinate activity of other brain centres when the child is forming a systematic plan of action. Since middle children attain greater proficiency at systematic planning during the same time as these changes occur in the frontal lobes, some experts infer that brain development is responsible for this improvement. When we suffer damage to the frontal lobes, we demonstrate a weakened ability to sustain our goals, we are more easily distracted, and we lose our concentration.

Near the end of childhood the brain attains about 90% of its adult weight. Growth in foresightful activity permits more effective transaction of rule-bound games. In addition, the right and left sides of the brain are bridged by neural connections in the corpus callosum, a linkage which brings language and thought into closer working units and engenders more effective classroom learning.

[7]**Differences in thinking abilities between early-adolescents and late-adolescents**. As we shall see time and again in the course of this book, an adolescent is not an adolescent is not an adolescent: The thinking abilities of the early-adolescent are dramatically under-developed when compared with the late-adolescent. The differences in mental functioning which separate "early" from "late" adolescents affects every phase of adolescent mental and emotional life. For example, as we shall see in Chapter Two, egocentrism exerts a more powerful impact on younger adolescents, while needs for intimacy and mutuality hold greater influence on older adolescents. The most significant differences are seen in perspective-taking, problem solving and decision making. In a nutshell, early adolescent are lacking in experience and development when compared with their older brothers and sisters. Here is how F. P. Rice summarized it:

> The early-adolescent has little recognition that decision-making activity involves clearly specifying goals, considering options, and checking before taking action to implement a decision. This conclusion is consistent with other research findings that young adolescents are less likely than older adolescents to generate options, to anticipate the consequences of decisions, and to evaluate the credibility of sources. . . . There is a significant increase with age among 12 to 18 years old in the ability to handle sophisticated decision making. Older adolescents formulate more options, pay more attention to future outcomes, consult more with experts, and are more aware of the implications of advice received from someone with vested interest. Other studies have identified such cognitive changes as improvement in memory and improved ability to process information and apply knowledge. (1999, p. 61)

The most profound consequences of the cerebral differences among younger and older teens are social rather than academic. As we shall see in Chapters 9 through 12, many complications are associated with younger-older teen relationships.

Two

The Self in Adolescent Thought

It is well to remember that the entire universe, with one trifling exception, is composed of others. (John Andrew Holmes)

The mind is not a computer even though it has computer-like qualities. The mind, and all it produces, operates in conjunction with, and under the surveillance of, the self. Psychology, which likes to boast of its accomplishments, is in an awkward position when it comes to explaining the self (what is it? what are its origins? how does it engage in dialogue with itself?) and its relationship to the mind, thought and intelligence. When it comes to understanding the self and its relationship to the human thought process we really have more questions than answers.

Egocentrism is part of the mystery which baffles psychologists. I, too, am baffled, and I don't plan to be unbaffled in the near future. Like most psychologists, I try to explain egocentrism without explaining the self.

In very general terms, egocentrism is the mental force which causes one to think and feel *from one's own point of view* without taking into account other perspectives and other feelings. It is, by definition, narrow and self-driven. Its purest and perhaps most natural form is seen in the innocent narrow-mindedness of young children, the youngest of whom are so egocentric they do not even know that views and perceptions different than their own even exist. (This obliviousness in toddlers and preschoolers is part of their charm, their candor, and their innocence.)

Egocentrism is an inevitable fact of how the human mind works. No thinker, young or old, completely escapes its force. The difference between mature and immature thinkers is found *in their strategies for dealing with their own egocentrism*. Young children, since they are unaware of their own thought process, have no posture toward their own egocentrism. They are, so to speak, ignorant of their own subjectivity, and impervious to their own mental operations. Mature thinkers (which most adolescents are most of the time) are able to take a stance in regard to their egocentrism. They know their thought process works in a self-protective way, and to counter-balance this tendency they double-check and re-assess their own thinking to minimize egocentrism.

21

No one completely transcends egocentrism, but mature thinkers use mental strategies to keep it under control.

Jean Piaget, probably the foremost thinker on this topic, described egocentrism as an *embeddedness* in one's own point of view which colors everything from the inside out. In young children this embeddedness exists without their awareness; hence, they un-self-consciously think that what they saw at the parade is the same as what everyone else saw, and they presumptively infer that the scenes in the movie that made them sad made everyone sad. Egocentric children see the world from their own position in it without realizing that it is a position, and therefore, they are *egocentric through ignorance of their own subjectivity.* (Ignorance of one's own subjectivity, by the way, is not unique to children, but in them it is created by an intellectual immaturity *natural* to their developmental age. Ignorance of one's own subjectivity during adolescence has completely different causes.)

Ignorance of one's own mental operations is part of the child's mental ecology, and it is not until the onset of formal thought (at about age 13) that much progress is made in overcoming it. As we saw in the previous chapter, one of the great mental advances of adolescence is the ability to analyze one's own thoughts and thus to acquire greater mastery of one's own mental operations.

• • •

Very young children give the impression that they don't know that perceptions of reality other than their own exist. Suppose, for example, that a three-year-old knows candy is hidden behind the books on a bookshelf and then another child (who does not know this secret) enters the room. If an adult were to ask the first child what the second one thinks is on the bookshelf, the first child will usually answer "candy." Because the first child knows candy is behind the books, he can't imagine the other child not knowing. (This of course is not the case with five-year-olds, who have an increasing grasp of private knowledge.) Piaget understood the young child's egocentrism as an innocent absence of self-consciousness, and this is a helpful way to look at young children's thinking.

Margaret Donaldson adds a deceptively simple passage: "the child does not appreciate that what he sees is relative to his own position; he takes it to represent absolute truth or reality – *the world as it really is*" (p. 20). The failure to recognize that what one sees is relative to one's position is the trademark of egocentric narrowness whether it occurs during childhood or adolescence.

Children are both victims and beneficiaries of their egocentric narrowness: victims because they cannot stand back to evaluate their own thoughts, and therefore are at the mercy of them; beneficiaries because egocentrism provides clarity and organization, without which children would be swept away by the swirl of infinite data their minds are charged with assimilating. As a mental operation, egocentrism is both an asset and a liability, but as one faces increasingly complex problems which demand objectivity and impartiality for an effective solution, it becomes an increasing liability.

To think as a child is to have one's thought dominated by egocentrism; to think as a mature thinker is to possess mental strategies which assess the influence of egocentrism. All thinkers are egocentric to some degree, but children more than adolescents, and adolescents more than adults.

Childhood and Adolescent Egocentrism

Jean Piaget believed that the first two decades of life see four distinct stages of egocentrism, three during childhood and one during adolescence. His research on egocentrism captures its age-bound qualities, and provides a glimpse of the different roles egocentrism plays at different ages. Each stage of egocentrism builds upon the advances of the previous stage, each contains its own method of reality analysis, and, importantly, *each contains unique modes of reality distortion.* As we would expect from even a cursory knowledge of childhood, each of these stages is associated with advances in mental development; but, each stage is also characterized by a particular differentiation *failure* which is not overcome until the child progresses to the next stage. Let's take a quick look at these four stages to prepare for future discussions.[1] From birth to about age two, the thoughts and actions of very young children are grounded in a radical egocentrism so complete as to make it virtually impossible for them to differentiate the self from the larger world, (an idea akin to, but not the same as, Freud's concept of primal narcissism). Egocentrism at this age is based upon the child's "belief" that sensory impressions are essential to the existence of the object. Sensorimotor egocentrism begins to decline when the child recognizes that objects have their own existence independent of his (or her) perception of them. This, in essence, is the child's first acknowledgment of the "as-is" world. Transcendence of this egocentrism arises from the emerging capacity for mental representation.

From age two to about age six, the child has difficulty differentiating between symbols and their referent. The child does not seem to understand the relationship between the signifier and what is signified because symbols are viewed as identical to their referents. The egocentrism of this age causes youngsters to leave out important information in speech and thought. When trying to "master the symbol," the child often assumes that particular words carry much more information than they actually do.

When symbol and referent are confused, as is the case with children from two to six years, thinking about the world *is always in terms of one's position within it.* Children at this age believe that their perspective is shared by others, because it does not occur to them that another one is possible, which is to say that they believe that their understanding of an event is, for all intents and purposes, the only one possible.

From age seven to about age eleven, the child can perform elementary reasoning and submit concrete hypotheses for testing. These abilities transport the child beyond the more primitive comprehension of younger children, but, on the other hand, they also introduce new deficiencies in the thinking process. For example, children at this age do not understand that their hypotheses need to be thoroughly and fairly tested to determine whether they are true, or likely to be true. At this level of egocentrism children accept that their own hypotheses are generally true and, interestingly, that facts should adapt to fit their hypotheses. Which is to say that reality should accommodate to them rather than the other way around. (As we shall see later, this reasoning holds a certain fascination a few years later during adolescence). Its allure is simple: it requires the world to adjust to "me" instead of "me" adjusting to the world.

The egocentrism inherent to this stage makes it difficult for seven to eleven-year-olds to differentiate between perceptual events and mental constructions; hence, they do not tend to think independently about their own thoughts, another way of saying that they do not hold their mind accountable to its own creations. However, with formal operations (about age twelve or thirteen) this form of egocentrism diminishes and passes the way of most childhood thinking.

Children in this stage of egocentrism are not wise to the fact that errors take place within the thought process itself; this imperviousness to their own mental operations has one bright side, it empowers them to believe in the rightness of their thinking even when it is filled with errors, particularly errors of omission. Narrowness of thought enhances certainty of conviction since the mind does not entertain sufficient data to recognize that more than one conclusion may be deduced from that data. (For this reason ten-years-olds may be totally certain of their beliefs on, for example, abortion, but by age fifteen, because their thinking is more comprehensive, less so).

From age twelve to about age twenty, youth progress through the final great stage of egocentrism. In this stage the power of formal thought comes into play, one consequence of which is that egocentrism is placed under the microscope of analytic thought. "Formal thought" is a synonym for the higher plane of intellectual functioning which blossoms during adolescence and which allows the young person to reason more accurately, to conceptualize more objectively, and to think more systematically. Chapter One described the particulars of formal thought in considerable detail; therefore, we will not go further into it here. The egocentrism of adolescence (despite the presence of formal thought) expresses itself in many ways, and each, in its own way, moves the adolescent away from analytic thinking toward egocentric thinking. This "moving away" from formal thinking toward egocentric thinking carries profound consequences for the adolescent day-to-day thinking habits, and for fascination with things pertaining to "me" and "mine." Indeed, the adolescent's intermittent adventures in egocentric thinking are among the most fascinating (and limiting) aspects of their intelligence.

The Increase and Decrease of Egocentrism During the Teen Years

Current research supports the idea that most adolescents undergo a gradual migration away from the extreme egocentrism which dominates the thinking of children. Generally speaking, egocentrism lessens with each advancing year. Therefore, one of the gravest concerns that we have for late-adolescents as they approach graduation from high school, or as they prepare to leave for university or assume their first full-time job, is that they have not yet lost the egocentrism which typifies early adolescents. To arrive at one's 19th birthday locked into the egocentric thinking patterns of a thirteen-year-old forewarns of a host of problems, not the least of which is moral emptiness.

We infer that egocentrism is lessening as a force within the intellect when sociocentric tendencies take a stronger position in day-to-day life and when the individual experiences an ascendance of outside-the-self investments. The *causes* of egocentric decline are not clear. Psychologists have observed for decades that it is correlated with increasing age, but age itself does not account for it, because even though most adolescents decrease in their general egocentrism, some become *increasingly* egocentric, narcissistic, and selfish with each successive adolescent year.

When we look at the behavior patterns, thinking habits, and emotional focus of late-adolescents, we see how they are less egocentric than younger teens. For example:

• Late-adolescents perceive more accurately the traits which define their personal uniqueness; as a result their need for fables and fictions lessens.

• Late-adolescents are developing their own standards of self-importance; therefore, self-evaluation goes beyond the standards of family and peers; late-adolescents do not think well of themselves simply because they are well liked by their peers.

• Late-adolescents perceive the positive and the negative aspects of their nature; their identity is freer from transient influences – they are more capable of enduring commitments.

• Late-adolescents are more adept than their younger brothers and sisters at *perceiving the unique personhood of others,* forcing them less frequently into stereotypes. They see more clearly the individuality of parents and relatives, and for this reason adults find them easier to get along with than younger adolescents who, for the most part, lack insight into the adult personality.[2]

• During late-adolescence the trend is toward more continuous investments, partly in response to increased cultural demands for long-term decisions regarding issues such as job and marriage, and partly in response to a personal identity more secure with itself and more certain about what is meaningful in the long run. This deepening of interests precipitates greater interest in "larger" issues, and mapping out long range goals. A general humanizing of values takes place when youth of this age create their value system out of their growing understanding of their own feelings. All this accords with an *expansion of caring,* a growing empathy, and a greater concern for the feelings of others.

• During late adolescence there is a greater tendency to identify oneself in terms of belief and ideology. Late adolescence is an age for coming to grips with the necessity of commitment; a realization facilitated by the intellectual ability to see beyond immediate concerns.

• During late adolescence youth become more committed to the long-term calendar.

Since the 1980s the differences which separate early-adolescents from late-adolescents have become of increasing concern to all professionals in the "youth-industry," especially educators and psychologists. This concern springs from our recognition that even though both age groups are part of adolescence, younger adolescents remain generously laced with the mental and emotional residue of childhood, while older adolescents are invigorated with the mental and emotional anticipation of early-adulthood. Our willingness to grant greater responsibility (and accountability) to youth as they grow through adolescence is based, in serious measure, on our expectation that egocentrism weakens significantly during this time. The bottom line: adolescents cannot advance in their social and cognitive maturity until they lessen in their egocentrism.[3]

Egocentric Speech

Egocentrism influences all facets of adolescent life. In the next chapter I will describe how egocentrism shapes the adolescent belief system, how it persuades youth to think that society should be reformed to better gratify their own particular needs, and, finally, how it encourages the fable of immunity. Here, however, I want to discuss how speech is shaped by egocentrism.

The speech of three, four, and five-year-olds is so egocentric that it almost always reflects their own immediate perspective, their own immediate desires. Their use of language is so privately grounded that they often use words and symbols completely meaningless to everyone else. Indeed, the very young child makes no attempt, in the words of Piaget, "to place himself at the point of view of his hearer." It is not even clear that four-year-olds have a conception of what a "point of view" means. Since their communications are self-based, preschoolers may speak right past each other without paying any attention to what kids next to them are saying. Elementary teachers know it is impossible to communicate effectively with first- or second-grade children without first sharing their frame, seeing with their eyes, for these children cannot climb out of their own frame to see through the eyes of the teacher.

Young children assume that the listener will accurately decode the meaning of a statement, even when it lacks the vital information needed to provide proper meaning. (Anxious adolescents make the same assumption). Thus the child may blurt to mother "She dropped it on him," without explaining who "she" is, what "it" is, or who "him" is. Mothers understand these sentences by adding the necessary information the child left out; which, of course, they do with remarkable facility. But the sentence, unto itself, is egocentric in every regard. Informational speech, (speech by which precise information is conveyed) remains primitive in proportion to the speaker's egocentricity. Egocentric speakers are weak at informational speech because they do not effectively separate the information they are communicating from their reaction to it. They don't report, they editorialize.

Before we look at adolescent speech, we should make clear that adolescents are effective conversationalists in most situations, especially non-threatening ones. In most settings their command of the rules of conversation (known as pragmatics) is commendable; they take their turn in conversation far better than children, and they are usually able to recognize when speech might be lost in the hubbub of confusion or distraction. They know how to use questions to convey commands (Why is everyone talking so loud at the dinner table?); how to deploy articles such as "the" and "a" in ways to enhance understanding (She is the person to see if you want a job); and how to tell stories, jokes, and anecdotes to entertain guests of varying ages. Despite these allocentric qualities, their speech is also encumbered with egocentric and narcissistic peculiarities, and they are the focus here.

Margaret Donaldson hit the mark perfectly: "For a conversation to go smoothly, each participant needs to try to understand what the other knows already, does not know, needs to know for his purposes, wants to know for his pleasure" (1978, p. 18). Donaldson's "listener-based" communication shares a good deal with what H. P. Grice called "effective communication," which is governed by four maxims:

• The maxim of quantity: Speak neither more nor less than required.

• The maxim of quality: Speak the truth and avoid falsehood.

• The maxim of relevance: Speak in a relevant and informative way.

• The maxim of clarity: Speak so as to avoid obscurity and ambiguity.

These maxims represent standards no one can meet all the time. They are standards of speech we try to meet when information needs to be conveyed accurately and honestly. *Egocentric* speech is incompatible with effective communication because it places maximum emphasis on self-concern, and minimal emphasis on objectivity and impartiality. In effective communication fairness and accuracy are presumed, and when it cannot be presumed, effective communication is thwarted. (This is why, for example, the speech of children is inappropriate for legal trials, and why children's stories must always be verified and confirmed.) Effective speech is listener-grounded, egocentric speech self-grounded; effective speech takes into account the listener while egocentric speech takes into account the speaker.[4] In sum, egocentric speech does not impede the production of words, sentences, or paragraphs, nor self-expression and first-person narrative, but it does, in a serious way, impede effective communication.[5] [6]

During the course of the adolescent years egocentric speech typically decreases in frequency and declines in power. When a decline in egocentric speech does not occur by late-adolescence we suspect developmental delay, we anticipate an increase in narcissistic tendencies, and often we observe a reluctance to accept the responsibilities of approaching adulthood. Perhaps the most positive thing we can say about egocentric speech is that it keeps the growing person centered in the self, and helps the person to face challenges that can otherwise be overpowering.[7]

Getting the Upper Hand on Egocentrism

Egocentrism is always present in the thought process, but it is not a constant presence. The issue is not that some individuals have no egocentric thought – that is impossible; the issue is that some individuals have learned how to check its influence while others have not. The hallmark of the mature thinker, as far as egocentrism is concerned, is knowing when egocentrism is influencing one's thought process and when it isn't, and then, to engage mental strategies which assure that objective thought is not swept away by egocentric thought. Immature thinkers have no such awareness and few mental strategies, consequently, thought is swept away by egocentricity more frequently and more convincingly.

Egocentrism subsides when the thinker learns to double-check the mental conclusions which present themselves to consciousness. "Present themselves" is critical. Younger children accept their mental conclusions without much awareness that they spring from *the thought process itself*. Children treat mental conclusions as facts of nature. They simply are, and what they are is. Thoughts are not double-checked because children tend not to grasp the relationship between process and product: which is to say that they do not understand how conclusions work their way through the thought chain. They don't recognize the self-centered quality of their own thought; indeed, as suggested earlier, younger children don't seem to even recognize that degrees of egocentricity exist; therefore they cannot think of themselves as more (or less) egocentric than anyone else, or as anyone being more (or less) egocentric than themselves.

Adolescents are more advanced. They know that conclusions derive from mental processes, and they also know that these processes are not error free. From these insights into their own thought process, they eventually learn how to double-check and to verify their mental conclusions. From the moment that one realizes that one's own thought process is prone to error, and that errors can be discovered and corrected, young people begin to live in a dialectical relationship with their own intelligence. Thought no longer merely "presents itself." It is inspected, analyzed, evaluated, accepted, and rejected. Thought is business; thought is taken seriously; thought passes judgment on itself; thought challenges the self to evaluate its egocentric nature.

Egocentrism persuades the thinker to accept an idea by whether it agrees or disagrees with what "I" want, or with what "I" need, a persuasion which wrecks objective analysis and impartial thought; as much as any single force, egocentrism contributes to the fables, the illusions, and the ineffective speech of adolescence.

• • •

One may assume that egocentrism is losing its influence on thought, speech, and behavior when the adolescent begins:

• to recognize that others have a private existence that parallels "my" existence, and that others have rights which parallel "my" rights.

• to recognize that adults possess their own private individuality, and their own unique history; when adults are not perceived as merely part of the impersonal "other."

• to lessen demands that others always see things from "my" point of view.

• to understand that they share important commonalities with others; when the fable of complete singularity begins to fade.

• to join social gatherings without assuming that their arrival carries great significance.

In my experience over many years of working first-hand with teens, I have found that very few *early* adolescents attain much distance from their egocentric nature; *middle*-adolescents master several of the above indicators, but rarely all of them. *Late*-adolescents exhibit a far greater facility, and are thereby transported away from the intense egocentrism of their younger brothers and sisters. Indeed, this march away from egocentrism is one reason older adolescents can think philosophically and scientifically, and, as well, can be such good counselors to younger teens.

Final Comments: How Egocentrism Shapes Adolescent Thought

> Egocentrism makes it difficult for the individual to differentiate between how things ought to be and . . . how things are. (Rolf E. Muuss)

If a more pressing issue than egocentrism exists in adolescent psychology it has eluded me. Egocentrism shapes every aspect of adolescent life, especially the ability to understand oppositional views, and to perceive contexts greater than the context of self.

To assist those readers who seek a brief overview of the major ideas put forth in this chapter, the following summary is provided.

• Egocentrism is an *embeddedness* in one's own point of view; an entrenchment which makes it difficult to understand the ideas or appreciate the interests of others. Its "pure" form is expressed in very young children, who reduce all experience to their own point of view without any apparent awareness that this is what they are doing. Its "contaminated" form is expressed in adolescents, who reduce all experience to their own points of view even though they have the mental ability to be aware that this is what they are doing.

• Late adolescents are less egocentric in thought, behavior, manners and morals than early adolescents. They perceive more accurately the traits which define their uniqueness; they are more accepting of the positive and negative aspects of their nature; they possess greater ego identity and they see more clearly the individuality of parents and relatives; they experience a deepening of interests, partly in response to increased cultural demands for long-term decisions, such as about job and marriage, and partly in response to greater certainty about what is meaningful in the long run.

• The "conquest" of egocentrism means that one perceives in increasingly accurate terms the thoughts, moods, and emotions of others.

• We assume that egocentrism is in decline:

When the adolescent begins to perceive adults as individuals with their own private individuality.

When the adolescent recognizes that the rights of others exist on the same plane as "my" rights.

When the adolescent accepts that it is impossible for another person to completely understand what it is like "to be me."

When the adolescent ceases to demand that others always accept his (her) point of view.

When the fable of total singularity begins to lose power.

What we do not fully understand is why *most* youngsters become less egocentric during their adolescence, while some become more egocentric; why most youngsters become increasingly clear in their thinking, while others become increasingly beclouded; why most youngsters become more accurate in their social perceptions, others more distortional; why most youth show a decline in fables, while others show an increase; and, finally, why some youth expand in sharing and cooperation, while others harden into a narrow selfishness.[8]

With these unknowns beckoning, we are now ready to embark upon a deeper look at how egocentrism shapes the mental and emotional life of teens.

Anecdotes and Supplemental Information

[1]**The predictability of egocentrism**. My intent here is not to claim that egocentrism follows the clear-cut paths which Piaget believed, but to indicate that it is predictable in its progressions, and lawful in the force it exerts on the thinking process.

[2]**A late adolescent's perception of her parents.** Here is how a 21-year-old university student described the changing relationship with her parents during adolescence:

> Yes, my attitude toward my parents did change during adolescence. As I became older, more mature, my thoughts and perceptions of them were more positive, much more positive. At a younger age, when friends were of extreme importance, and the attitude shared was that parents were more enemies, that were "old" and "didn't know anything." I considered my parents "uncool," at times embarrassed to be with them. I refused to see their side in an argument or suggestion, [I was] unhelpful, questioned things – why did I have to do this or that. As I became older, my parents were my best friends and still are. I took a complete turn – now I *want* to hear their advice or suggestions, I respect their advice as well as decisions, I help not only with perhaps physical labor but emotional support, I like talking with then, learning from them, etc.

[3]**Perspective-taking and its relationship to age**. R. L. Selman, perhaps the most influential spokesman for the developmental progression of perspective-taking, claimed that children grow in their perspective-taking through a series of successive stages. He argued that each stage is qualitatively different from the preceding, that each level develops in sequence, and that most children mature through these progressive levels in approximately the same time frame.

Selman's ideas offer helpful instruction on the child's migration away from egocentrism since perspective-taking and egocentrism exist in a converse relationship, that is, as one increases the other decreases; therefore, to know about one is to know indirectly about the other.

Age three to six years. The guiding principle of the most primitive form of egocentrism, the kind manifested among one-year-olds, for example, is "You see what I see, you think what I think." At age three, children recognize that other people disagree with them, but they have only minimal understanding of the basis for another person's point of view; they recognize the existence of their own thoughts, and the thoughts of others, but often they confuse one with the other. Even by age six, most kids don't think that another person could respond to the same situation differently than they did. Their understanding of others is blocked by a poorly differentiated understanding of themselves.

Age five to nine years. At this stage children understand that their interpretations of a social situation may be the same as, or different from, another person's interpretations of the same situation. They are aware that different people process information differently, and therefore, that they draw different conclusions, which is itself a considerable childhood achievement. In Level 1 children are able to think from another person's perspective in a very limited fashion. The most significant feature of Level 1 is the child's recognition that each of us formulates ideas through our own individual thought process. At this stage children still cannot judge their own actions from the frame of reference of another person if that frame is different from their own. Another feature of this level of perspective-taking is that children realize that others hold different perspectives, but they naively believe that everyone will agree once everyone is given the same information. Since they don't recognize the role of private thought in evaluating information, they mistakenly conclude that information itself molds conclusions. Hence, they have difficulty anticipating when disagreements will arise, and how disputes are resolved.

Age seven to ten years. A further advance in perspective-taking occurs when children attain the ability to see their own feelings and actions from another person's perspective. This allows them to anticipate other people's judgments of their actions more proficiently than in Level 1. Therefore, in addition to realizing that others have different perspectives, children now recognize that others can appreciate their perspective. Children now recognize that two people may disagree even though the same information is available to both. Most children at this stage still cannot think about their own point of view and the point of view of others simultaneously.

Age ten to thirteen years. This level witnesses the ability to step outside a two-person exchange and imagine how a third person might perceive the interaction. This extension of perspective-taking permits looking at an interaction from two perspectives simultaneously (my own and my parents', for example). In essence, Level 3 allows the child to think about how another person is thinking about him (or her). (It is a necessary precursor to the formation of the Imaginary Audience).

[4]**Effective and egocentric communication.** In the culture of children, effective communication takes a backseat to egocentric communication. Effective communication increases in direct proportion to the exactitude (and significance) of what is being communicated, and in the need for precise statement and exact summary, i.e., "Your pay will be $8 per hour, and you will begin work at 0730." Egocentric speech increases in direct proportion to the felt need of the speaker to say something, and to the power of the spoken word to draw focus to oneself. Both forms of speech are vital, but they serve different purposes in different settings.

[5]**Egocentric speech.** Marlene Webber (1991), who spent two years in the streets of urban Canada interviewing runaways, relates a telling tale of harmless, though typical, adolescent egocentrism. In preparing to conduct an interview with a young man,

one of dozens whom she interviewed for her book, she had gone to great lengths to explain to him that in her book no names would be revealed, that anonymity would be maintained throughout, and that, in disappointing fact, because of time and space constraints, most of the youngsters she interviewed would never even be included in the book. After these ground rules had been carefully established and agreed to by the young man, an interview followed. Upon its conclusion a friend of the young man arrived; he was introduced to the author with typical egocentric panache: "This is the lady I told ya about that's gonna write a book about me" (p. 9).

[6]**Adolescent vocabulary**. Adolescent's are prone toward a vocabulary of extremism; they persistently misuse words such as never, always, every, none, nobody, everyone, totally, completely, and forever.These words make any situation appear more grave than it is, and when they are taken literally, as they often are, they impose an urgency which chokes clear thinking. Related to this, fabled thinking is also propelled by a vocabulary of extremes, helping it to gain lift much easier than with the lower octane vocabulary of moderation.

[7]**Egocentrism and conversation.** Egocentric speech tends to lessen when the self is acknowledged or consulted on a regular basis. Genuine self-acknowledgement dampens the clamor for excessive expression.

[8]**What we don't understand about adolescent egocentrism.** We do not plan to abandon the reader on these important topics – most of them are given full hearing in upcoming chapters. For example, Chapter six looks into the reasons why teens have so much trouble thinking clearly; Chapter three deals with why adolescents are attracted to fabled thinking, and how it inclines them to make judgment errors when they are engaged in at-risk behavior; Chapters Seven, Eight and Nine deal with adolescent selfishness and its bearing on the emotional health of teens.

Three

The Fictional and the Fantastic
in the AdolescentThinking Process

It is natural to man to believe true what he desires to be true, and to believe it because he desires it. (Arthur Schopenhauer)

In Chapter One we discussed the higher reaches of adolescent intelligence, including the ability to think scientifically and philosophically, rationally and systematically, introspectively and comprehensively. All of these abilities combine to produce an adolescent thinker *capable* of an impressive intellectualism. In Chapter Two we shifted our focus to the self and to egocentrism in order to see how they influenced adolescent thought. Now we are ready to investigate some of the malfunctions within the adolescent's thinking repertoire, especially the tendency to participate in fictional, fanciful, and fabled thinking. Adolescents don't invent flights of fantasy, but they do things with them not evident during childhood or adulthood. Some are harmless and eccentric, others are devastatingly self-diminishing. Whatever their consequence, they are a force in the adolescent's mental repertoire, and, not infrequently, they seriously undermine the powers of formal thought and the higher reaches of adolescent intelligence. At-risk behavior, self-destructive behavior, and self-diminishing behavior are all encouraged by the fables of adolescence.

A fable is a brief narrative which makes edifying points through animals that speak and act like human beings, as in *Aesop's Fables*. This is not our usage. In our usage a fable is a self-serving deception, or an irrational conclusion which better allows one to follow one's desires and inclinations. In fables, belief supercedes reality, and facts are bent to fit one's ends; "bent," not "broken," since fables must have an appearance of truth. A fable that is obviously false or blatantly stupid is not of much use to anyone. A fabulist, therefore, is an inventor and a creator of semi-truths. Fables are not a sign of mental illness, they do not even suggest a fundamental malfunction within the perceptual process – especially as far as adolescents are concerned.

Fables are not unique to adolescents, and it is delusional to pretend they are. Adults and children also engage in fabled thinking, and their capacity for it is well documented in the literature of personality psychology. But here we are solely concerned with the fables of adolescents because they are, in structure and genesis, different than the fables of children and adults. My intent here is to explain how age-based, developmental processes encourage fabled and fictional thinking during adolescence.

Adolescent fables have a unique quality in that they are creations of an intelligence grander than anything known to childhood, yet, at the same time, an intelligence weighed down by a need for protective armor not usually seen in childhood. Adolescent fables are a mix of intelligence and protection, and an unpredictable mix at that, but their impact on thinking is fairly predictable – they encourage adolescents to misperceive the actions of others, to misunderstand the motives of others, and, to misread their own individuality.

With fables we get a bit closer to the edge than we prefer. The risk is that we will begin to think of adolescent thought as shamanistic or magical, and this is not so, not even close. The adolescent thought process is not *governed* by fables, but it is predisposed to them, especially when they are socially advantageous, or narcissistically comforting. The opposite extreme is the belief that adolescents are, at bottom, completely rational thinkers who easily produce orderly and coherent thought. This also is not so, and, in all likelihood, never has been. Accepting that adolescents are naturally rational inclines us to believe that adolescent fables are learned, or imitated, or somehow picked up from the peer group. While it is true that some are picked up from outside sources, most fictional and fantastic thought originates within the mental operations natural to the adolescent thought process.

Thus far three points have been made which we will draw upon in future discussions:

• fables are not unique to adolescents, they also exist in the mental life of adults and children;

• adolescents are predisposed to create fables; a predisposition which is tempered by the *capacity* for formal thought and rational thinking;

• some adolescent fables are learned from others, but most fables are *created* by processes inherent to the adolescent thought process.

•　　•　　•

Certain researchers claim that the fables come into existence from lack of education. This is not right. Fables are constructed from the mind's intrinsic creativity, and nourished by the adolescent's (and the child's) predisposition to create narcissistically comforting conclusions. Good education helps young-sters to double-check and re-think their fables, even to discard them, but lack of education does *not account for their existence.* In the simplest possible lan-guage, fables are a natural product of the adolescent thought process.[1]

All fables possess a believable element or they cannot pass the inspection of even a modest intelligence; fables shade and darken the truth, enhance and inflate the truth, but they never completely destroy it. A fable must be believ-able or it is a mere absurdity. As Massimo Piatelli-Palmarini says in his excit-ing work *Inevitable Illusions,* "There is always some truth in any illusion; there is always some persuasion in a fallacy" (1994, p. 31).

The fables described in this chapter are not intended to be false and phony portraits of how a small percent of teens think; rather, they indicate how the thought process bends and shapes reality to better fit the adolescent's needs. Fables, for the most part, are created without conscious intent. Despite the plausibility of some fables, they are rarely convincing in the face of a healthy skepticism, and this is one reason adolescents prefer uncritical companions who won't dismantle their fables. The fables described in this chapter occur with such regularity in the community of teens that they can be thought of as normal in the statistical sense of that word, but they can also be thought of as abnormal (unhealthy) when they lead to destructive outcomes.

When we talk about the adolescent predisposition to create fables, we are not breaking fresh territory. In the 1920s Jean Piaget reported that the adoles-cent thought process *periodically* operates as though the world should bend to it rather than it to the world (a remarkable testament to the power of narcis-sism in the thought process), and that they also sometimes seem to accept that the world should submit to their own idealistic views rather than to the systems of reality upon which they already operate (Piaget, 1928).

But enough of these preliminaries. It is now time to see how fables come to life in the adolescent's rich and fertile intelligence. We are drawn to five basic fables: the fable of the audience, the fable of total uniqueness, the fable of invincibility, the pregnancy fable, and the idealism fable.

The Fable of Performing Before an Audience

> For, when they come together, each young person is an actor to himself or to herself and a spectator to everyone else. (David Elkind)

Teens sometimes do not know for sure when they have an audience and when they don't, a confusion of no small consequence to their day-to-day lives. For starters, the thinking of many adolescents is stamped with the pre-sumption that people are paying attention to them when they are not, and that they are concerned about them when they are not. Here is one way to think about this basic confusion and how it blurs social perceptions.

> . . . the adolescent is continually constructing, or reacting to, an imaginary audience. It is an audience because the adolescent believes that he will be the focus of attention; and it is imaginary because, in actual social situations, this is not usually the case. . . . The construction of imaginary audiences would seem to account, in part at least, for a wide variety of typical adolescent behaviors and experiences. . . . When the young person is feeling critical of himself, he anticipates that the audience . . . will be critical too. The adolescent's wish for privacy and his reluctance to reveal himself may, to some extent, be a reaction to the feelings of being under the constant, critical scrutiny of other people. (Elkind, 1967, p. 1030)

The sense of always being evaluated produces within the adolescent an exaggerated self-consciousness similar to what adults experience during a job interview; a blistering self-consciousness which causes them to mold every sentence just so, to elicit the desired reaction from the interviewer. As the adult is on stage in the job interview, so the adolescent is on stage before peers, parents, and passers-by. One 20-year-old, describing his adolescent years to me, recalled: "I was obsessed with the thought that everyone was always watching me. I was always conscious about what I was doing, just in case someone was watching and would sometimes do things just because someone was watching (or so I thought)."

The imaginary audience excites a sense of being outside and inside the self at exactly the same instant; two selves in the same body, one acting while the other is watching the act.

> I was always conscious of how other people saw my reactions. It was as though there were two of me. One part was living my life, feeling happy and sad, excited and disappointed. The other part was outside of me watching and noting my effect on others. The outside part enjoyed getting sympathy, attention, and praise. It could romanticize even the worst situations. It put me in the place of the injured heroine from the movies. It was the part of me that imagined what people would say about me if I were to die, and wished to be involved in tragedies for the effect of it. The inside of me did the feeling. .(Garrod, et al., 1992, p. 176)

•   •   •

The imaginary audience is no mere regression to the fantasy life of children. Children do not have the mental capacity to construct the complex imaginary audiences which adolescents assemble routinely. The imagination of children, while vivid and exciting, cannot negotiate the complex demands of an imaginary audience. The imaginary audience, as we are here describing it, cannot come into being until the onset of formal thought and the range of intellectual skills which come with it.

The main point about the imaginary audience is the fact that it is imaginary, not real. *What young adolescents can do, and what children cannot do, is create such audiences in their head.* Where the young adolescent has difficulty is in recognizing the subjectivity of his or her own mental constructions. The young teenager has trouble in differentiating between the concerns of others he or she has created and concerns which are properly his or her own. So, the fact that children can infer the thoughts or feelings of others given the situational context, does not really speak to the issue of the imaginary audience, which is mental construction and not social reality (Elkind, 1985).

All of which brings us to our final point: the intellectual complexity of the imaginary audience is well beyond the mental range of children – it simply cannot unfold until the intellectual powers of adolescence are in place. Sophisticated, fully developed fables do not come into being until formal thought has enriched intellectual capital; adolescent fables are born of higher order intelligence, and for this reason they are hard for the adult to refute, and difficult for the adolescent to disregard.

The Fable of Total Uniqueness

When I say `I' I mean a thing absolutely unique, not to be confused with any other. (Ugo Betti)

The tendency to think of oneself as completely different from everyone else on the planet is called "the fable of total uniqueness." This fable grows out of the premise that one's experiences are more profound, one's thoughts are more advanced, and one's fears are more intense than anyone else's. Because of this fable it is thought that no other person can know the pain of my suffering, can comprehend the profundity of my convictions, or imagine the depths of my love. "I" am a sun unto myself, completely unique, totally singular. Under the influence of this fable it is not a wonder that teens feel hopelessly isolated from the rest of us.

From their special perch youth come to believe that they see what others cannot, and experience passions grander than anything known to their friends, teachers, and most assuredly, their parents. This misperception prevents them from recognizing what they share with others, and encourages an obsession with the particular at the expense of the universal. This fable prevents youth from seeing how the principles of love and life which apply to others also apply to them.

The uniqueness fable is based on the presumption that "I" am so unique that no one could possibly grasp my thoughts, or fathom the depth of my emotions. The first fable we discussed, the imaginary audience, places the adolescent on centre stage in direct view of knowing eyes, while the second fable, the uniqueness fable, places him in leprous isolation from an audience of strangers who could never understand him even if they tried. These fables disorient the self in relation to others, and create a frustrating confusion about one's role in the social order, the family order, the school order, indeed in every order.

A final point: the adolescent's heightened self-awareness makes him (her) acutely sensitive to matters of individuality, hence all issues pertaining to "me," "mine," and "myself" assume tremendous significance. The uniqueness fable is the perfect seasoning for this acute sensitivity, as it proclaims "I" am not merely an individual, "I" am the quintessence of individuality.

The Fable of Invincibility (Also Known as the Fable of Invulnerability)

> . . . the extreme risk taking of certain youths requires neither coercion nor ignorance of the likely consequences. William Gardner

The issue is not whether teens are risk takers, because we accept as a starting point that they are. Whether we are talking about the '50s "chicken" players in their hot rods speeding toward each other on a collision course, or the '90's "surfistas" riding on the top of high speed commuter train cars in Rio de Janeiro with high-voltage wires inches above their heads, the risk-taking habits of adolescents are no rarity. Indeed, there has never been a culture, to my knowledge, where adolescence is known as a time of *reduced* risk taking. In North America, for example, mortality rate increases by about 200% from early to late adolescence, the single largest percent increase in any two consecutive age cohorts in the life cycle; injuries account for most of this increase. Death rates from motor vehicle injuries increase by about 390% (in Canada 58% of *all* traffic accidents involve sixteen to twenty-one-year-olds, and in the province of Alberta, during 1995 one-half of all motorcycle deaths involved drivers *under* the age of eighteen); homicide by about 590%, and other unintentional injuries by about 75% between early and late adolescence. Other forms of risk-taking are also evident; for example, one in seven adolescents in the U.S. have contracted a sexually transmitted disease, a level twice as high as for people in their twenties, even though the twenties population is much more sexually active than the teen population. (See Irwin, 1993, for further data on this topic.)

At-Risk Behavior During the Teen Years

The emphasis in this chapter has been with the motives and mental habits which encourage irrational thinking and counter-productive behaviour during adolescence. The *urgency* of this topic, however, cannot be understood without an awareness of at-risk behavior in the teen population. The following information speaks to this topic.

Alcohol use. Most research indicates that alcohol is the most commonly used substance among teens. Health Canada (1995) and Statistics Canada (1996/1997) report that alcohol consumption among teens is a significant health issue in all Canadian Provinces. The percentage of students reporting alcohol use is surprisingly consistent – 56% for New Brunswick, 54% for Nova Scotia, 52% for PEI, and 57% for Newfoundland (Poulin, 1988).

Out-of-school teens consume more alcohol than teens attending school. Anderson (1993) reported that 88% of out-of-the mainstream youth were identified as regular users of alcohol – about 15% of these youth were daily users.

Consuming five or more drinks per drinking sessions constitutes high-risk alcohol use. About 65% of youth who are alcohol users report consuming more than five drinks in one setting each month. (Consuming 5 drinks greatly increases the probability of vehicular death or injury). About 25% of grade 7 –12 students report being a passenger in the past year with a driver who had too much to drink. (About 700 000 teens are passengers in a car driven by an impaired driver at least once per year.) More 15-19-year-olds Canadians die as a result of car accidents than from any other single cause. Alcohol is a determining factor in more than half of these deaths.

Tobacco Use. Among Canadian teens, cigarettes are the most common substance used daily. Approximately 28% of males, and 30% of females between the ages of 15 and 19 are current smokers (Galambos,et al., 1998). In the Atlantic provinces the incidence ranges from 33% in New Brunswick to 37% in Newfoundland; of those who smoke, almost half smoke daily. Out-of-the mainstream youth are more likely to be smokers (about 75% of these youth smoke), and heavier smokers - 52% of them smoke more than 25 cigarettes per day (Anderson, 1993).

Cigarette smoking, even more than alcohol consumption, is positively correlated with health problems during and immediately following adolescence.

Illegal drug use. Virtually all research investigating the habits of Canadian teens confirms that marijuana is the most commonly used illegal drug. It is easily available in all rural and urban communities, and in virtually every public high school. Health Canada (1995) reports that slightly more than one-third of 15-24 year olds have used marijuana. In the Atlantic provinces, about 30-35% of high school students have used marijuana in the previous year. Magic mushrooms (psilocybin/mescaline) and LSD were used by about 10% of students during the previous year. Estimates are that about 6% of teens have moderate to serious problems with drugs other than alcohol. (This amounts to approximately 1.5 million teens in Canada). Among drug users, about 15% report that drugs adversely affected school work and exams, and 5% reported trouble with the police as a result of drug use (Poulin, 1998).

The use of crack cocaine is showing a dramatic upswing in the adolescent population. "Addiction experts from across the country say crack cocaine is fast becoming a fixture in rural and small town Canada, and its users are getting younger." Experts report "a huge increase in the use of crack cocaine in the last three years. It is probably one of the most addictive drugs we've seen." Crack is manufactured by melting powder cocaine and adding baking soda. The mixture is cooled and hardened into a "rock," which is smoked in a pipe and produces a high that lasts 20 to 30 minutes. Symptoms of crack cocaine use include paranoia, agitation, and violent behavior, posing a risk to both the user and the crisis worker (July 24, '00, The Canadian Press). Youth workers report that teens, during the experimental stage of crack use, almost always report that they can handle it, even though they see peers on a daily basis who couldn't and can't.

For further information on at-risk behavior among teens see [11] at the end of this chapter.

The puzzle of educated risk-taking. All risk-taking is not impulsive. Much of it is thought through and calculated – even though the calculations may be more flawed than the thinker recognizes. The at-risk behavior of intravenous drug users is a good example. In their investigation of intravenous drug users in Alberta, Ann Marie Pagliaro and Louis Pagliaro (1993) found that many of their subjects have a relatively high level of knowledge of HIV/AIDS. The authors conclude that among the more than 800 drug users they interviewed, knowledge about how HIV is transmitted is fairly sophisticated. *Nevertheless, users perceive that their own risk of contracting HIV is very low despite the fact that they are participating in high risk drug use and sexual behavior.* They recognize the risk-in-general, but not the risk-to-me. According to the Pagliaros, these individuals believe that what they know somehow does not apply to them, they "harbor illusions of unique invulnerability" (1993, p. 12). These illusions interest us not only because they endorse high-risk behavior, but also because they exist side by side with objective knowledge and intellectual awareness. Illusions do not live in isolation, they cohabit with the higher reaches of adolescent intelligence – with formal thought. The trademark of adolescent fables and illusions is that they are constructed, and defended, with the full cooperation of formal thought. (In Chapters Five and Six we will investigate why formal thought does not always follow the path paved by reason, rationality, and formal thought.)

Fables of immunity observed among North American teens

- Pregnancy will never happen to me.
- Car accidents will never happen to me.
- Drug addiction will never happen to me.
- Alcohol addiction will never happen to me.
- Cigarette smoking and tobacco chewing will not harm me.
- The police will never arrest me.
- Marriage problems will never happen to me.
- The usual consequences of behavior do not apply to me.

The research findings of the Pagliaros support the findings of Moore and Rosenthal, who investigated adolescent attitudes on the same topic. "This is a common theme among heterosexual adolescents in their responses to the threat of AIDS, the `not-me' myth. It is clear that most adolescents have not personalized the risk of HIV/AIDS, *perceiving the illness as a threat to others, not themselves.*[2] This is consistent with the belief that adolescents' thinking is characterized, in part, by the "personal fable" (1993, p. 128). Then, to further show how illusions increase risk-taking, Moore and Rosenthal observe:

Adolescents' belief that it "can't happen to me" has been shown to influence risk-taking in a variety of health-related situations including smoking and contraceptive use. In a recent study of British adolescents, Abrams *et al.* (1990) found high levels of concern about the presence of the HIV virus in the community *but little evidence of concern about their own levels of risk.* (1993, p. 129)

Defying the improbable. The attitude of invulnerability is not as irrational or as impulsive as some psychologists make it out to be. For the most part, it involves defying the unlikely, and confronting the improbable; but in most instances the odds are in the adolescent's favor. We all do this kind of thing. When we speed through a just-turned-red light, when we drink too much before driving home, when we fudge on our income tax, we are risking penalty, but at a level of probability we are willing to chance. Teens follow a parallel line of logic, if we can call it that, in their invulnerability fables, but the difference between adult and adolescent invulnerability fables are twofold. First, the adolescent's range of experience is so limited there is a limited ability to *estimate the likelihood* that negative consequences will follow a particular action. Second, the adolescent's capacity for future analysis is too weak to accurately *calculate the price "I" must pay* for defying the odds. (Reckless driving, diving into water of undetermined depth, and the use of guns to settle disputes are examples of adolescent behavior which are clouded by the invulnerability fable).[3]

The dangerous aspect of the fable of invulnerability is that it encourages the *continuous and on-going defiance of the improbable*, and as we know, every unlikely event will eventually occur given enough chances. What we usually discover in the vulnerability fables of adolescents is defiance when peer acceptance or peer rejection is at stake. When these conditions are factored out of the equation, teens can be remarkably clear thinkers.

I have one final comment on the adolescent tendency to defy the improbable, to engage in risk behavior. When thought is not consequence – aware, action is not consequence – inhibited. The failure to think through the consequences of one's action does not cause that action; but, importantly, the action has no chance to be inhibited by thought. Failure to think does not cause impulsive or stupid behavior, it merely keeps it from being inhibited, vetoed, over-ruled.

Pregnancy Fables

"Pregnancy doesn't run in my family." Sixteen-year-old girl's response as to why she doesn't use contraception.

No adolescent fable has more significance to teens (and to society-at-large) than the fable which asserts "I" will not become pregnant. The pregnancy fable is perhaps the most complex adolescent fable, as it requires the acceptance of certain truths and the rejection of others. It is a classic fable in its composition and a nightmare in its outcome.

The pregnancy fable is one of an adolescent's most durable because it is bolstered by the invulnerability fable (others become pregnant, but I will not), by the uniqueness fable (my love is so unique that it could not result in an unwanted outcome), and by egocentric idealism (if I do have a baby it will be perfect, as will my relationship with it). The pregnancy fable is reinforced by fidelity (the impulse to bond), and particularization (the belief that one's love is caused solely by one's love partner). All of these fables take place at a time of life when the girl is experiencing her sexuality in a richer and more profound way than ever before, when she is searching for her own sexual identity, and when she is trying to figure out the emotional peculiarities of her boyfriend. Thus, while the fable itself is rather straightforward, the mental dynamics which create it are not. As a further reminder, this fable is tremendously age-influenced. Ten and eleven-year-olds, for example, hold almost no pregnancy fables, neither do twenty-five to thirty-year-olds. They are nearly universal, however, among early and mid-adolescent North American girls.

One sixteen-year-old I interviewed was convinced that she would never become pregnant, despite having unprotected sex with her boyfriend "more than several times" per month, because, in her own words, "pregnancy does not run in my family." However, while espousing her invulnerability to the consequences of sexual intercourse, she refused to drink alcohol because of the increased risks it posed while driving, she refused to smoke cigarettes because they increase the risk of disease, and she refused to experiment with drugs because she did not want to risk being arrested. All of these struck me as reasoned, calculated viewpoints, cohabiting with pregnancy beliefs ill-reasoned and laced with denial. This uneven reasoning is everyday fare among adolescents. The lesson to be learned in all this is that fabled thinking, like temper tantrums, binge eating, and moodiness, *appear in episodic bursts.* They are not permanent qualities of the adolescent personality – more like uninvited visitors.

Most young people have a friend, or parent, suffering the calamities from which they claim exemption. These human tragedies are not denied in their totality, and to perceive adolescent denial in this way is to miss the overall picture. Rather, the adolescent acknowledges these tragedies as facts of human life, but facts which affect me differently than everyone else. Why? Because "I" live by different rules, different probabilities, different consequences. Why am "I" different from others? Because "I" am so completely unique that rules, probabilities, and consequences do not apply to me. (When this line of thinking turns even more selfish – it evolves into the entitlement attitude of the narcissistic style – see Chapter Nine for further analysis).

The conclusion that presents itself in this matter is that adolescents have trouble assessing probable outcome. While this might, on first glance, seem harmless, it is not. The failure to assess *probable* outcome contributes to adolescent mortality, to adolescent unemployment, to adolescent drug use, to adolescent gang membership, to adolescent runaways, and of course, to adolescent pregnancy.[3a]

Nothing is more disastrous to adolescent life than the inability to predict the outcome of one's actions, and fables contribute to that inability.

Consider that almost all pregnant teens report being surprised at finding themselves pregnant. (A. Phoenix, in her investigation of young mothers, reports that 82 % of pregnant adolescent girls had not planned to get pregnant.) When adolescent girls are asked how they planned to avoid pregnancy, a stunning range of fables emerge.[4] For example:

• the belief that they did not have sex often enough to become pregnant;

• the belief that they did not experience an orgasm, and therefore, could not conceive;

• the belief they were "too young" to become pregnant;

• the belief that they would not be "caught" during high risk days (even when they understood the ovulation cycle);

• the belief that it couldn't happen to "me."[5]In a superbly documented investigation of adolescent sexual behavior, which Eleanor E. Maccoby of Stanford University described as "by far the best thing that's been written on the subject," Susan Moore and Doreen Rosenthal (1993) make pertinent observations on the adolescent thought process and its understanding of the relationship between pregnancy and contraception. They report:

> In some ways, these young women are reminiscent of the 'invulnerable' adolescents. . . . These are young people who believe that they are unlikely to suffer the negative consequences of their actions, and hence take risks that others would not (p. 149).

The authors then go on to report that Littlejohn, in her Australian research, "found that 20 per cent of pregnant teenagers did not think they needed to use contraception because they couldn't get pregnant" (1993, p. 149). Upon close inspection, one usually discovers that these beliefs are not acquired from friends, from parents, or from TV; they are neither copied nor stolen. Rather, these beliefs are the creation of a mental process which manufactures protective fables and comforting illusions when the mental process must investigate emotionally charged topics.[6]

"Teenagers are not able, as a rule, to be mature and responsible about sexual relating." (Lauren Ayers)

All thinking about pregnancy is not fabled. But this does not mean that it is reasoned and objective, nor that one can talk about it openly with one's boyfriend. Thinking about pregnancy does not necessarily convert to action, or even to discussion.

> I didn't ask him about it and he didn't ask me about it. It was really strange because I was terrified that I was going to get pregnant. I always thought about it, worried about it, *but I couldn't do any thing about it.* Although we didn't use contraception, and we didn't talk about it, I thought about it constantly, and I was scared. I even wrote a paper about teenage pregnancy for a psychology class. I remember working on it thinking, "This could be you, you have to do something about this." I remember having this feeling that I HAD to talk to him about it, but I couldn't. It seemed easier not to say anything and put it out of my mind, to try to forget about it. (Garrod, et al., p. 252)

Perhaps things are not really this complicated. Perhaps girls become pregnant simply because they cannot restrain themselves when they are sexually aroused. Perhaps their thinking is not fabled, merely over-ruled by lust. Among early- and middle-adolescent girls this explanation is lacking because, according to youngsters themselves, the sexual act is not emotionally over-powering. During the early years of adolescence, intercourse almost always has to do with something beyond the sexual. It is expressed sexually, but sexual desire is not the dominant cause.[7]

> Pleasure does not appear to be a driving force in a teen girl's decision to become sexually involved with a boy; rather girls seem to enter into the relationship as a rite of passage that they must undergo. When a girl says that she feels it's time that she had sex with a boy her decision does not stem from unrestrainable passion. (Ayers, 1994, p. 163)

If not from passion, from what? That is the question to which we have not as yet discovered an acceptable answer. Our ignorance is based on the fact that youth themselves do not know with certainty why they engage in sexual intercourse, and equally perplexing, they don't know with much certainty why they *abstain* from sexual intercourse.[8]

The Fable of a Pure and Lofty Idealism

> A fantasy is always more satisfying and credible if someone else can be made to believe it. (Karl Meninger)

Like their elders, adolescents dream of greater things and better days. These dreams spring from their intelligence, their idealism and their egocentrism, but the mix is never easy to determine. Much of what passes for adolescent idealism is "false" and "incomplete" because the thinking process which produces idealism is routinely swamped by its own egocentricity. Hence, the idealism of youth is real but not pure. This is a small matter when you recognize that self-enhancement plays some role in every idealistic system, but a great matter if you are one of those adults who naively believe that youthful idealism is grounded in open-eyed objectivity.

Perhaps nowhere is this seen more clearly than in the idealism of youth who Inhelder and Piaget called *idealistic reformers*. Idealistic reformers claim that they want to transform society in order to make it better, but the real motivation behind their desire is to better satisfy their own needs, desires, and cravings.

> . . . the adolescent not only tries to adapt his ego to the social environment but, just as emphatically, *tries to adjust the environment to his ego.* In other words, when he begins to think about the society in which he is looking for a place, he has to think about his own future activity and about how he himself might transform this society. The result is a failure to distinguish between his point of view as an individual called upon to organize a life program and the point of view of the group which he hopes to reform. (1958)

Ideology is the system of ideas, beliefs, and attitudes which make up a world view; it is the doctrine which guides political and cultural plans, and provides the strategy for putting them into operation. An ideologue is one who adheres to, believes in, and advocates the truth of a particular system of thought. The power of ideology (as far as the adolescent is concerned) is in its power to explain mystery and to resolve contradiction, and, in this regard, it holds the same attraction as myth and illusion.

Idealistic reformers, as one might predict considering their egocentric motives, are attracted to an ideology which justifies their desired reforms, and which better serves their needs and desires. Something of a dependency circuit exists here since reform cannot take place without an ideology to guide it, and ideology cannot guide without reformers to put it into action. Here the connection is forged: youth are drawn to the coherence of ideology and ideologues are attracted to the energy of youth. Youthful idealistic reformers and older ideologues exist symbiotically, each filling a need of the other. In today's society, it is pretty much axiomatic that wherever one appears so also does the other.

All youthful idealism is not deficiency driven; to claim that it is not only makes one a psychological determinist, but worse, a cynic. Yet, to deny the existence of self-serving idealism in the adolescent's thought process is to deny part of the belief system which guides their day-to-day life.

Final Observations on the Fables of Adolescence

> There is in human nature generally more of the fool than the wise. (Francis Bacon)

And while he didn't, Francis Bacon could easily have added: "And what is true for human nature, is more so for adolescent nature."

We have been concerned with two central themes. The first has to do with *how fables are created* in the adolescent mind, and the second has to do with the specific content of these age-driven creations. It has been emphasized throughout that fables are not mere *divertimenti* in the adolescent's mental ecology, and that they carry profound implications in day-to-day behavior – especially the pregnancy fable ("I will not become pregnant"), and the immunity fable ("I will not experience the negative consequences associated with this behavior.") Fables cause youth to miscalculate the probability that certain events will (or will not) occur; they distort reality and twist one's relationship with it.

We are still very naive, of course. We really do not have a very polished understanding of the adolescent thought process and we are not terribly enlightened about the origins of their brightness *or* their dullness. But we do know that adolescents are predisposed to fables – a predisposition which contributes more to their dullness than to their brightness. Like all myth and fantastic legend, fables mix the natural with the supernatural, the real with the greater-than-real. They stand halfway between wishful thinking and the simple assumption of good fortune. The importance of fables to the lives of ordinary adolescents is indisputable. I say "ordinary adolescents" because I do not want to convey the impression that fables occur only in deviant or disturbed youth; fables are part and parcel of the adolescent thought process. All adolescents, quite obviously, do not subscribe to all of the fables described in this chapter and some adolescents don't subscribe to any of them; but all adolescents, at one time or another, subscribe to certain fables.

In this chapter I overviewed several fables which subtract from the adolescent's ability to understand the world as it is, including:

• the fable that one is being watched, evaluated, scrutinized and, in general, the object of everyone's attention when this is not the case – the fable of the imaginary audience.[9]

• the fable where the adolescent unduly exaggerates singularity, fails to recognize the commonalities shared with others, and views himself (herself) as a solitary island in an indifferent sea – the fable of total uniqueness.

• the fable of personal invulnerability (sometimes called "the invincibility fable," or "the immunity fable") leads the individual to believe that the laws of probability and the rules of common sense do not apply to "me." This fable gains momentum when the individual is emotionally charged, when desire is peaked, and when self-gratification is on the line. This fable is situation-grounded and emotion-driven rather than free-floating. Fables, after all, are exceptions to the adolescent's *tendency* toward rational thinking and objective analysis; they are aberrations in an otherwise powerful thought process.

• the fable that negative consequences will not accrue from sexual activity. I called this the "pregnancy fable," but it could as easily have been called "the AIDS fable," or "the STD fable," or "the immunity to consequences fable."

• the fable of a pure and lofty idealism imbues the young person with the belief that their ideals are bigger and better than anyone else's, and that the reforms suggested by them are in e*veryone's* best interest. This fable does not acknowledge that one's idealistic reforms are grounded in one's own needs, desires, and fantasies.

• the fable that those who believe in "me" and "my" reforms are themselves noble and worthy.

I have tried to indicate how a feeling of unease cloaks these fables because the objective portion of the adolescent's thought process usually recognizes that they are, at bottom, fiction, but this awareness is not enough to reason them out of existence. It is encouraging to learn that fables do not remain convincing to the adolescent forever, and that most of them are discarded or outgrown, but convincing they are in their moment.[10]

Anecdotes and Supplemental Information

[1]**Fables and intellectual distortion**. In human perception distortion takes many forms, and in this chapter we describe only a few. In general, distortions occur when we see others in light of our own needs, desires, and fears. Most typically, these distortions yield three basic outcomes, all of which, to greater or lesser degree, degrade clarity of thought.

• They endow others with characteristics they do not have, or have only to a minor degree.

• They cause the perceiver to be blinded towards positive assets in others, such as friendship or devotion, or, cause the perceiver to be blinded toward liabilities such as lying or exploitation.

• They result in the perceiver's being clear-sighted toward certain behaviors within others, and having a keen alertness to certain positive or negative traits. This "clear-sightedness" is focussed into specific domains for reasons specific to the perceiver, and as a result, they preclude an overall perspective. These distortions are not blatant misrepresentations but subtle re-arrangements and realignments.

[2]**Adolescent misperception.** Arnett (1992) claimed that adolescent thinking is influenced by "a probability bias" in which youth accurately assess other people's susceptibility to a set of conditions, but do not associate themselves with the same susceptibility. Sometimes called "gambler's perception," because gamblers who fully understand probability often make the same mental error.

[3]**Is the fable of invulnerability real?** Some research findings do not support the existence of the fable of invulnerability. A number of researchers have questioned whether it is a plausible explanation for adolescent risk-taking.

Elkind argued that adolescents' personal fable involved a notion of uniqueness so strong that it "becomes a conviction that he will not die, that death will happen to others but not to him." Elkind noted that his theory was largely speculative, being based entirely on anecdotal evidence from his clinical patients. *Quadrel, et. al., in their analysis of the adolescent personal fable claim that* [there was] *minimal systematic evidence supporting the theory.* (1993, p.103)

They summarize their findings this way:

The most straightforward account of these results is that adults and teens rely on similar, moderately biased psychological processes in estimating these risks . . . both cognitive and motivational processes could contribute to exaggerating one's safety. On the cognitive side, for example, the precautions that one takes (or at least plans to take) should be more visible than those taken by others, especially for active events (where control is more possible). . . . On the motivational side, wishful thinking might deflate perception of personal risk. . . . (Quadrel, 1993, p. 112).

In some quarters it is believed that once adolescents understand the relevant facts pertaining to any particular risk they will avoid exposing themselves to that risk. Those who accept this point of view believe that when teens take risks they do not truly comprehend the danger, either because they do not have the mental power, or because the appropriate information has not been given to them, or it has been delivered in an ineffective manner. Another interpretation is that adolescents understand risks but choose to ignore them. They may consider the risk acceptable, given the benefits, or they may enjoy the thrill or social status that comes with it.

[3a]**Adolescent irrationality.** At this moment in time, early into the 21st century, we really do not possess any comprehensive explanation of adolescent irrationality. Our understanding of why so many teens (especially mid-adolescents) become pregnant even when they have learned the mechanics of contraception is not much more advanced today than it was 30 years ago. Neither do we understand why sexually active young women (19 to 23-year-olds, for example) efficiently avoid pregnancy while sexually active 15-17 year-olds do not, and our understanding of why teens are so influenced by fads, trends, fashions and why they are so pathetically molded by pop culture is no more advanced today than it was 30 years ago. Our understanding of why teens shoot and kill one another is no more advanced today than it was 30 years ago. In sum, even though we describe and document irrational acts more precisely than we did in the past, we really have not, as yet, come up with explanations which account for this irrational behavior. Part of the answer, I believe, is found in the adolescent thought process, particularly in the fables and fantasies of this age.

[4]**Girls.** We know more about the thinking of girls because of their accessibility to research in programs specifically designed for pregnant teens. (It is widely believed by researchers that boys – especially early- and middle-adolescents – are quite unreliable in their sexual reporting. The usual tendency: boys of this age over-report their sexual behavior, girls of this age under-report.

[5]**It won't happen to me.** This is especially true in teen pregnancy. For example, McGuire's investigation of teen pregnancy is titled *It Won't Happen To Me: Teenagers Talk About Pregnancy.*

[6]**Are teens sexually irresponsible?** Lauren Ayers expressed it as straightforwardly as anyone. "A young teenage girl has neither the wisdom nor the experience to handle the risks of sexual activity, and the statistics bear out the damage done to young females. The foresight, responsibility, and integrity required for responsible sex come only with maturity and cannot be made to develop earlier." (1994, p. 64)

[7]**Teen pregnancy.** No one has thus far advanced a convincing explanation as to why so many teen-age girls become pregnant when they don't want to be pregnant. But one thing is crystal clear: teens do not think clearly when it comes to sexual intercourse. Their behavior is neither policy-driven nor consequence-driven. The higher reaches of adolescent intelligence are surprisingly inept when sexually active youth try to monitor and regulate their own sexual behavior. (These same youth are often quite effective in managing and regulating other aspects of their daily lives – school work, employment, etc.). If ever there existed a need for effective intervention in the lives of teens, this is it. Unfortunately, on this topic the thinking of adults is as distorted as the thinking of teens, though for completely different reasons.

[8]**The morality of abstinence.** By grade 10 almost all teens have learned to give to themselves, and to those who ask, morally elevating reasons for their own sexual abstinence, even though they do not always give the same reasons when they are trying to explain the sexual abstinence of others.

[9]**The self as paranoid.** The thought that one is paranoid yields a fascinating, yet bewildering, return to the adolescent thinker because it encourages (and justifies) protracted self-examination – an inherently pleasurable adventure. If this strikes you as puzzling, test it in action. Ask an adolescent you know well if he ever thinks he is paranoid. If the conversation flows naturally, without being steered, you will most likely observe that the adolescent does not walk away from this idea, or even view it scornfully; rather, the idea proves intrinsically fascinating because it provides the opportunity for the self to investigate itself and then, for dessert, to talk about itself. If your adolescent friend doesn't know the meaning of the word "paranoid," the same results are obtained with the word "weird."

[10]**Self-deception.** All fables include a dose of self-deception. And despite the growth of formal thought during adolescence, one of the ironies of mental progression is *as mental abilities increase self-deception also increases.* With increasing age children grow in cognitive ability, gain in awareness of their social environment, and develop the ability to put themselves in the position of observer. The net effect, according to Feldman and Custrini, is that:

> children come to understand that they can fool both themselves and other people. This is due to their growing realization that discrepancies can exist between their inner experience and their outer appearances. They come to see that they have greater access to their inner psychological experience and thoughts than do other people, and consequently are in a position to manipulate the appearance they present to others. (1988, p. 41)

From these primitive beginnings self-deception penetrates daily routine, leading to the conclusion that self-deception *inevitably* increases with age:

> In sum, there is a cogent argument to be made for the position that self-deception will become more pronounced with increasing age. The research on other-deception shows quite clearly that children become increasingly successful in being deceptive nonverbally toward others and in identifying . . . when others are being deceptive. As children's understanding of other-deception grows, however, they are more likely to understand their own instances of self-deception. If this is the case, they are forced to use increasingly sophisticated defense mechanisms to protect themselves. Ability in self-deception, then is likely to increase with age. *It is ironic indeed that the increased skills in understanding others may act to decrease one's awareness of oneself.* (p. 51)

All of which gives us cause to re-examine Ludwig Wittgenstein's observation: "Nothing is so difficult as to not deceive oneself."

[11]Further information on at-risk behavior of Canadian teens.

Sexual activity. Sexual activity carries health risks and pregnancy risks during adolescence. For Canadian youth, the consequences of sexual behavior are as costly as alcohol use, tobacco use, or drug use. Sexual intercourse during adolescence is age-influenced; in virtually all teen communities the percent of teens engaging in sexual intercourse increases slightly each year between ages thirteen and twenty. (Hence a greater percent of sixteen-year-olds are sexually active than fifteen-year olds, seventeen-year olds than sixteen-year-olds, etc.)

In Canada, about 55% of all youth 15-19 are sexually active, with about half of these reporting having sexual intercourse during the past year – while about 80% of youth aged 20 to 24 reported having intercourse during the past year (Lindsay, 1994). Recent research indicates that about 26% of 9th graders, 37% of 10th grade, and 58% of 12th graders had engaged in sexual intercourse in the previous year (Poulin, 1998). The increased number of *early* adolescent sexual activity is of great concern to Canadian health officials, and. of course, to the parents of teens, and to teens themselves. Sexually active youth are at considerable risk for sexually transmitted disease. Females between 15 and 19 have the highest rates of gonorrhoea and chlamydia infections of any age group in Canada. HIV infection has shown a dramatic increase among youth since 1998.

Without question, however, the greatest medical, personal and societal consequences of teen sexual behavior are associated with pregnancy. (See [3], [4], [5], and [6] at the end of Chapter Eleven for further information on the consequences of teen pregnancy.

Eating disorders. Eating disorders are most frequently observed in females, but they are so widespread in the adolescent community that they require a moment here. About 30% of Canadian teens report binge eating, and about 20% purging. A persistent correlate of binge eating and purging is body dissatisfaction and perceived overweight, and because each of these is greatly influenced by self-perception, teen eating disorders are viewed differently from those of children (rare) and those of adults (not as rare). Bulimia nervosa typically has its onset in late adolescence, with an occurrence in girls about 10 times higher than that of boys. *The Diagnostic and Statistical Manual of Mental Disorders – IV*, estimates that from one to three percent of the *entire* population suffer from eating disorders (American Psychiatric Association, 1994). However, most research investigating teens places the incidence near 9% or 10%.

Multiple at-risk behavior. At-risk behaviors tend not to occur in isolation; on the contrary, they frequently occur in clusters, increasing their potential for damage. For example, many teens participate in alcohol consumption, cigarette smoking, illicit drug use, and sexual intercourse. Each of these behaviors carries a certain risk, but the risk is compounded when they co-occur. Teens who engage in multiple at-risk behaviors, for whatever reasons, are also at increased risk for legal problems and school problems. For example, among teens illicit drug use is associated with an increased incidence of violent delinquency, and an increased probability of carrying a weapon in public. Alcohol and illicit drug use increases the probability of being incarcerated for fighting or assault. Health Canada reports "a positive association between level of alcohol use and sexual activity and between alcohol use level and the likelihood of having unprotected sex" (1995). (As indicated earlier, unprotected sex creates significant health risks in the teen community.) Dropping out of school, or being expelled from school, is correlated with excessive alcohol and tobacco consumption – although the cause of this relationship is not clearly understood.

What causes teens to engage in multiple at-risk behaviors is not our focus here, but, in passing, we must mention that teens who engage in at-risk behavior are aware that they place themselves in some danger by their actions, but this awareness does not cause them to terminate the dangerous behavior. This mystery (why teens knowingly engage in behavior detrimental to their health and well-being) captivates our attention throughout this text.

(The information contained in this overview of at-risk behavior was greatly enhanced by an as yet unpublished paper, "Health Risk Behaviors and Identity Formation During Adolescence." The principal investigator for this paper was Dr. Brenda Munro, and the co-investigator, Dr. Maryanne Doherty-Poirer, both of the University of Alberta.)

Four

Why Adolescents Don't Argue Fairly

All of us, in our several ways, are illogical, irrational. (H. L. Mencken)

We all have our illogical and irrational moments, as it was H. L. Mencken's habit to remind us, and to admit it is not an indictment against our intelligence, but a statement about the *human* thought process. Therefore, when we claim that adolescents are characterized by a certain degree of irrationality, we have not levied a terribly serious charge against them, as it can be levied against anyone, or any group. Our concern here is not merely with the fact that adolescents have moments of irrationality, which they most assuredly do; rather, with how these "moments of irrationality" twist their reasoning and cause them to argue unfairly.

The difference between adolescents and adults is not that adolescents are irrational and adults rational, but that adolescents experience more frequent and more persistent episodes of irrationality. Adolescents experience episodes of confused thinking which trigger irrationality in their thought and in their behavior. In this chapter our concern is with how emotionality (and the faulty use of logic) contributes to the adolescent's habit of arguing unreasonably.

As far as thinking is concerned, adolescence is a time of intellectual industry and intellectual laziness, of penetrating insights and dopey platitudes. Trying to figure out how these contradictions work together in the same mind at the same time is the business of adolescent psychology. But, like so many mysteries of the second decade of life, they have not yielded much to progress. What is clear is that adolescent thought skips back and forth between calm reason and high emotionalism, and in skipping back and forth mental efficiency is reduced and accuracy is compromised in all areas of thought, including the ability to present a clear and coherent argument.

Anyone who lives with teens (or works with them) is fully aware of this skipping back and forth, alternating between calm reason and emotional ranting. This aspect of their thinking is frustrating not only to adults, but to teens themselves.

Jean Piaget was the first to observe that even though formal reasoning is available to teens *they often do not use it* because they lack familiarity with the tasks they are required to reason about. He also observed that the ability to reason does not exist on a one-to-one relationship with its expression; that is, to have reasoning is not necessarily to use it. "Individuals . . . who have this type of reasoning available in their cognitive repertoire, may, in fact, prefer to reason on a concrete level, *or not to reason at all in many situations.*" Furthermore: "it may be the case that although an individual has developed the competence to reason formally, the individual may not have developed the appropriate strategies or procedures to best access and apply this competence" (Overton, 1991). In other words, even though the adolescent may possess the intellectual raw material for clear reason, it is not always utilized completely, and sometimes it is not utilized at all. Which takes us back to questions we have dealt with before. "Why is it that adolescents do not use all of the mental abilities at their avail?" "Why do adolescents try to solve a problem with only part of their mental equipment?" "Why are adolescents, in certain situations, blinded to data others see clearly?" When we answer these questions we will know a great deal more about why adolescents have so much trouble negotiating fair and even-handed arguments.

Logic, Emotion, and Emotional Logic

Arguments are not exclusively determined by logic, or by one's proficiency with it, but they are greatly influenced by both. Let us, then, begin this discussion with a brief look at two types of logic available to the analytic mind (inductive and deductive logic), and one type which appeals to the emotional mind (affective logic).

Inductive logic is a method of reasoning by which a general law or principle is inferred from observed particular instances. It is the process by which we conclude that what is true of certain individuals is true of a class, that what is true of part is true of the whole, that what is true at certain times will be true in similar circumstances at all times. When a scientist infers that because a law holds in particular cases it must hold in the next, inductive logic is being used. When the government agrees to fund an inoculation program for the entire population because it proved effective with a sample population, this is an exercise in inductive logic.

Deductive logic works somewhat differently; it begins with a general premise and from it particular inferences are drawn, that is, reason flows from general observations to particular predictions. Deductive logic is reasoning where the truth of the premises determine the truth of the conclusions. Reasoning "If computers are used for business, then the cost of such a computer merits a tax deduction." "This computer is used for business," therefore, "The cost of this computer merits a tax deduction," is deductive reasoning. If the premises are true, they provide certainty that the conclusion is true. In sum, deductive logic is a process of reasoning where concrete applications are deduced from general principles.

The common denominator shared by inductive and deductive logic is that both require calm reasoning and comparative objectivity to work effectively. Inductive and deductive logic focus on the object of inquiry, assess by specified criteria, and demand objectivity of thought and clarity of definitions. In all these ways they represent formal thought at its best. I have introduced them to demonstrate the kind of thinking which opposes the emotive thinking discussed in the balance of this chapter.

Now we come to emotional reasoning, which I call "affective logic." Affective logic is thinking where the connection between judgments is emotional. "Susan is nice to me; she is good." Or, "I received a 'D' in Mr. Wilson's class; he hates me." In contrast to inductive or deductive logic, where truth is determined by measured comparisons and calm objectivity, affective logic is governed by cravings, desires, and fears. "There are too many students in the university; therefore we should keep minorities out."

Affective logic is not totally emotional or completely irrational – if it were it would have no believability whatsoever; rather, it blends rational thinking with emotional thinking under the pretense of objectivity. The persuasiveness of affective logic is not found in its coherence or its rationality, but in the thinker's belief that it is fair even though it is biased.

The charm (and the allure) of affective logic is that it fuses reason with passion. To think of it as totally irrational is to miss its essential quality. It is a mixture of reason and emotion, a blend of objectivity and subjectivity. Affective reason does not always produce false conclusions – it produces conclusions which the thinker deems true because of the purpose they serve; affective logic serves emotional needs not rational standards. Again, this does not guarantee false conclusions, only biased ones. At bottom, affective logic is about issues other than those actually being debated and discussed.[1]

Adolescents are predisposed to use (and respond to) affective logic for two reasons. First, their nervous self-consciousness impedes calm reasoning and impartial objectivity, making inductive and deductive logic difficult to sustain. (Prolonged calmness in analyzing an argument will often drive teens around the bend. Calmness obliterates their sense of urgency, while emotionality arouses and justifies it; this is why teens often equate firmness of conviction with intensity of expression, and conversely, calmness of expression with lack of conviction. A tendency, by the way, which is no small matter in determining for whom they will cast their ballot in an election.) Second, their experience in thought management, in sorting out the circumstances where emotion is likely to influence judgment, is limited and, for the most part, ineffective. In sum, lack of experience with logic, developmental immaturity, and high emotionality contribute to the adolescent's use of affective logic.[2]

The Head, the Heart, the Argument

Opinion is ultimately determined by the feelings and not by the intellect."
(Herbert Spencer)

One way to gauge the relative degree to which thought is shaped by reason or emotion is in the way an assertion is argued. When we observe how an
individual argues we learn a great deal about how one thinks.

An argument is a discussion in which reasons are put forward in support
of, or against, an opinion; in other words, an informal debate. In reasoned
arguments the participants attempt to demonstrate the truth or falsehood of a
proposition. An argument is a fair consideration or a reflection upon a problem which involves providing reasons for or against a matter of dispute. This
may sound more orderly than it is in real life. Arguments can be "won" and
they can be "lost," but in real life rarely does a judge arbitrate; participants
themselves decide the winners and the losers by standards which sometimes
have little to do with the argument itself. Indeed, among early adolescents, the
argument's victor is often determined merely by stamina, or by the claim of
one participant that he (she) won.

One educator said of high school students that ". . . their notion of debating is to say things louder and louder, rather than searching for some evidence
. . . Kids usually see things right away as either right or wrong, or look for
instant answers and tend not to go much further than that" (Lyons, 1990). This,
quite obviously, does not speak kindly to their ability to transact fair and honest arguments. Nor does it take into account how readily teens are able to learn
the skills required for reasoned argumentation when they receive good teaching and effective mentoring.[3]

The Art of Unfair Argumentation

The heart has its reasons which reason knows nothing of. (Blaise Pascal)

The key to arguing unfairly is to emotionalize, that is, to inject the argument with so much feeling and passion that the real object of discussion is lost.
To emotionalize defeats the purpose of a reasoned argument, which is to per-
suade by evidence and common sense. Arguments are supposed to be logical,
fair and honest, but when emotionalized they rarely are. In the course of emo-
tionalizing their arguments adolescents are drawn into an organic irrationalism
reminiscent of D.H. Lawrence's rant against reason: "We can go wrong in our
minds. But what our blood feels and believes and says, is always true . . . What
do I care about knowledge? All I want is to answer to my blood." Every adolescent finds himself (herself) sympathetic to Lawrence's plea for blood-truth.
Certainly there are moments when cerebral logic cannot slice through to the
heart of the matter, as every romantic chirpingly proclaims. As a guiding principle of the intellect, however, blood-truth is a disaster. And while D.H.

Lawrence may extol its virtues in matters of love and hate, he would not tolerate it for a minute in his banker, his cardiologist or his auto mechanic.[4]

We now come to the art of unfair argumentation, and this is tricky business where adolescents are concerned. Adolescents use strategies to "win" arguments, some fair some not – the unfair strategies are our concern for the moment. Unfair strategies almost always share the same purpose, and that is to emotionalize the topic, to aggravate the opponent, and to steamroll the fairness on which every honest argument depends. Here I would like to discuss six of the most common ploys youth use to derail an argument, or to turn it to their advantage. If you are a parent, a teacher, or an adolescent, you have seen them all before.

(a) Angering an opponent so that he (or she) will argue badly. Teens know that anger ruins an argument. This they have learned from personal experience, from observing parents and peers. Teens are gifted at engineering anger to their argumentative ends; to argue effectively with teens you must be able to master your own anger and cut through theirs.

"Of course you think I should be home before midnight, you are a woman-hating male." "You wouldn't understand being in love, you never really loved Dad." "What do you know about homework. You're just a construction worker who didn't graduate from high school."

Angering an opponent is made easier by the use of antagonizing definitions of everyday words. For example, defining "teacher" as someone who lets the student do whatever he (she) wants, or "parent" as someone who slavishly looks after the child's every need. Or, conversely, defining "teacher" as a lackey of administrative oppression and "parent" as a police officer. Using words confrontationally derails the real topic. (Many teens, in fact, consider this a "points" victory. "She really blew her cool.")

Adolescent arguments are about tension reduction and energy release as much as anything else; when teens argue calmly and dispassionately they not only lose their tenacity, they sometimes lose their convictions. Anger heightens energy and this is an advantage to an emotional thinker because emotional thinking requires energy to be sustained; logic, on the other hand, can be executed calmly and matter-of-factly. Teens, as a rule, have not mastered reason and to compensate for this lack of mastery they infuse emotion into their arguments to lessen the role of reason in the argument. When they argue with adults (or more skilled peers) by reason alone they all too often lose the argument. Most adolescents are not believers in reason, in great measure, because they themselves are ineffective in transacting it.

(b) Accepting or rejecting an idea because of its popularity with the audience.

Rejection and approval carry such force during adolescence that to twist an argument to avoid rejection or to gain acceptance is simply a matter of course in many situations. Because teens argue points about which they may hold no genuine convictions whatsoever, it is common practice for them to switch horses in mid-stream if they sense group disapproval for their point of view. (Teens may argue for no reason other than the visceral sensations and the emotional catharsis the argument creates).[5]

This tendency carries great weight in group discussions and "bull-sessions." Its value is that it shifts the focus from the points of the debate to what is accepted or rejected by the listeners. In sum, audience reaction is more important than the actual argument. (After all, it works for politicians).

(c) Using emotion to reduce the listener's concentration on the object of disagreement.

"Dad, I know you always want me to be happy and to do what is best for me. Well, quitting school and getting a job is best for me and will make me happy."

The manipulation of feeling increases as the adolescent increasingly understands how emotion influences the behavior and thoughts of others. (Teens know from personal experience how much their own thinking is influenced by fear and anxiety; it takes time, perspective-taking and formal thought to see the same principles working in others.) Hence, middle- and late-adolescents are rather adept at feeling manipulation while early-adolescents, who have not as yet developed a very sophisticated understanding of their own thinking habits, are less so.

(d) Disarming the opponent with charm.

This is really a subset of (c) but it is so widely used that it earns a place of its own. Albert Camus, the great existential thinker asked: "You know what charm is?" Answering himself: "A way of getting the answer yes without having asked any clear question." Charm is an attractive strategy for youth who have trouble getting the answer "yes" by reason or muscle.

The conscious use of charm to sway opinion is rarely seen in childhood. (Children may use charm to get what they want, but almost never to win an argument). For all intents and purposes, charm begins to flourish in the adolescent years. By early-adulthood many individuals have refined it to an art form. And, of course, it is vital to the human engineering of the successful narcissist. (More about that in chapters 10 and 11).

(e) Attributing undesirable motives to one's opponent.

Emphasizing the unworthy qualities of the opponent is a proven way to wreck an argument. "You hate Jason because he is white." "Why should I work? Your generation screwed up the world." This strategy is especially effective against individuals who feel that they must defend themselves against every attack on their character; it also works well against individuals low in security and high in inferiority – which means all youth some of the time and some youth all of the time.

Attributing undesirable motives to one's opponent is most likely to occur when the attributer is anxious or insecure. Since teens hold an anxious vigilance against dark and dangerous forces, they see evil where it does not always exist, especially in their argumentative opponents.

(f) Using emotion-laden words to deflect the topic.

"It is hard for me to talk about responsibility when it was you who divorced Dad and ruined our family." "Historians are all male chauvinist pigs who leave women out of their 'brave men and their heroic deeds' stories. It makes me sick." Or after parents discover drugs in the bedroom: "I can't believe you invaded my privacy. I feel like I have been violated."

Incendiary language keeps conversation hot. Teen-agers, while predisposed to this style of argumentation, are not its masters. This honor goes to daytime TV talk show hosts and political propagandists; not coincidentally, both have great success with adolescent audiences.

In conclusion, we have drawn attention to six strategies frequently used by teens to win their arguments, all of them "unfair" and contrary to the rules of reasoned debate, including:

- angering opponents so that they will argue badly;
- accepting an idea because of its popularity with the audience;
- using emotion to frustrate the opponent;
- using charm to win points;
- attributing undesirable motives to the opponent; and,
- using emotion-laden language.

Final Comments

"That is the happiest conversation where there is no competition, no vanity, but a calm quiet interchange of sentiments." (Samuel Johnson)

Why do adolescents emotionalize their arguments? Like so many questions in adolescent psychology, this one is easier to ask than to answer. But a few comments may be in order. The ability to assemble a good argument, and then to defend it against hostile questions (and questioners) takes years to develop. Even members of the high school debating team don't necessarily argue effectively with peers or parents. (Many individuals remain weak at this skill even after years of university education.) The ability to present an argument, to impartially analyze the data on which it is based, and to draw accurate conclusions from these data is a young-adult phenomenon. It is seen only sparingly during the earlier years of adolescence. The bottom line: adolescents are weak at arguing when arguments are bound to the rules of logic, evidence and common sense, therefore they bring in unfair strategies to enhance their cause.

The themes put forth in this chapter are an attempt to explain the primitive arguments so widely observed in teen circles. The task we have set out for ourselves (understanding the adolescent thought process and how it shapes their arguments) is frustrating because in one moment the adolescent may be reasoned and rational, the next emotional and confused. By now we fully recognize that adolescent thought is both rational and emotional, but in different measure at different moments. We wishfully think of adolescents as junior rationalists but few of them are; we are reluctant to admit that they make all of their important life decisions through an incomplete and immature intelligence.[6]

In addition to the impressive advances which dignify adolescent thought and push it to its higher reaches (which we have discussed at great length in Chapter One) we also observe a number of mental habits which distort and darken it. This chapter has shown some of the reasons why youth argue ineffectively, and how their tendency for unfair argumentation undercuts their intelligence and undermines their wisdom.

Anecdotes and Supplemental Information

[1]**Monitoring affective logic.** Affective logic flourishes in every climate of emotionality, and the specific emotion (anger, elation, love, hate) matters less than the intensity of the emotion. Individuals who monitor their thinking, may excuse themselves from a conversation when angry. "I'm too agitated to talk about this now. I'll say something I'll regret." As well, they may simply stay away from topics (or individuals) likely to incite anger. In this way they extricate themselves from situations where affective logic will likely prevail.

[2]**More on affective logic.** The affective logic typical of adolescence assimilates reality into the context of one's needs rather than accommodating one's needs to the context of reality. Even though affective logic is "normal" in that all teens use it as part of their thinking, it invites a host of mental habits which degrade objective thought. Affective logic is sometimes thought of as "thinking with the heart." Inductive and deductive logic is thinking with the mind.

[3]**Psuedostupidity and unfair argumentation**. David Elkind observed that adolescents sometimes seem to behave stupidly when, in fact, they are not stupid at all. Why is it, he asks, that when faced with a simple, straightforward question, adolescents

sometimes look at it from a dozen angles, mull it over and grind it up so thoroughly that they are unable to arrive at any reasonable solution? Why, Elkind asks, do adolescents often attribute devious, hidden motives to other people when none exist? Such mental convolutions are not the result of real stupidity but of "pseudostupidity." Elkind claimed that this kind of thinking is the consequence of accelerated cognitive growth combined with a lack of experience.

When adolescents acquire the more sophisticated reasoning skills which come with formal thought, they literally "think too much" about simple problems, about human motives, about anything and everything. As they gain greater experience and their thinking becomes more efficient, "pseudostupidity" disappears. Elkind's idea helps to bring into sharper focus some of the befuddlement of teen thought, but the thrust of his idea is not the same as what I am trying to describe. The concept of pseudostupidity is more specific than the impediments to critical thought created by affective logic.

[4]**Adolescent irrationality and "romanticism."** An interesting aside to this topic is how some adults wrongly perceive adolescent irrationality as a form of romanticism. Nothing could be further from the truth. The dominant currents of adolescent phenomenology are inherently antagonistic toward romanticism. One cannot be narcissistic and romantic. Narcissistic individuals are self-absorbed while romantics are life-absorbed; narcissists love themselves, romantics love life and that which honors life. When youth attain a sense of themselves in relation to the outside world they may, in the course of time, become romantics, or romantic in their outlook; until this moment they are romantic in word more than in deed, which, of course, means that they are not romantics at all.

To think of adolescents as "romantic" is to attribute to them qualities and sensitivities they are in the process of acquiring, but rarely have as yet integrated into their blossoming identity.

[5]**Arguing for the emotional arousal that it creates.** Sometimes an argument is made for no reason other than the visceral sensations it generates. The argument is merely the means by which emotions are aroused and vitalized. The argument is completely incidental to the emotive function it serves; accuracy, sincerity, and all of the argument's particulars are secondary to the heat created by the argument. Emotion-driven argumentation enlivens all youth exchange, adding to its vitality, its urgency, its charm – but little to its accuracy.

Psuedo-rage is when the purpose of rage is nothing more than to produce the self-arousal and the self-inflation that comes with rage. Friends may know when pseudo-rage is happening, but adults may have no clue because for them rage has an object – it is not an end in itself. Indeed, when adults misread pseudo-rage, believing it to be the real thing, they are mocked for being clueless to the situation. "Everyone knew he wasn't serious." "Get real. It was obvious that he didn't mean anything."

Witness tough-talk. "I could kill her." "I'm so fed up I could jump off a bridge." The truth is in the electricity of the statement, not in the exact words. This phenomenon should not to be lost sight of when we try to understand adolescent argumentation.

[6]**The "naturalness" of adolescent intelligence.** Adolescent intelligence, like child intelligence, cannot survive as it is; it must grow and expand to effectively han-

dle the increasingly complex problems it daily encounters. That intelligence must grow, however, does not mean that it does so automatically, or even that it wants to. The desire to grow intellectually is not natural to the adolescent personality. The willingness to negotiate the demands of clear thinking must be learned in the same way that a gymnast learns a back walkover on the balance beam – practice, coaching, repetition. And what is true for adolescent intelligence is equally true for adolescent argumentation.

[7]**Forces which distort adolescent intelligence: blind spots.** In psychological parlance "blind spots" refer to areas within a person's beliefs, attitudes or perceptions which are resistant to change through objective information or rational arguments. Blind spots leave a gap in our beam of awareness.

Blind spots lessen anxiety by trimming attention, and by sealing off painful experiences. Attention-dimming is the trademark of all young minds because attention-brightening illuminates too many unpleasant facts. Blind spots obliterate unwanted information and lessen anxious feelings; they are the par excellence dimming device, and they add immensely to adolescent imperviousness.

Blind spots prevent adolescents from accurately perceiving their performance weaknesses (such as poor academic achievement), their behavioral shortcomings (such as temper tantrums) and their character limitations (such as intolerance, prejudice, lying).

Five

Idea Manipulation

He admits that there are two sides to every question – his own and the wrong side. (Channing Pollock)

Maintaining perspective is a real problem where the adolescent is concerned, and even more so where adolescent thinking is concerned. If thinking expressed itself in even increments, or operated at the same level from day to day, our job would be much easier. No such good fortune. Adolescent thinking is frustratingly episodic, flashing and jabbing one moment, inattentive and lethargic the next; bold and bedazzling when analyzing, for example, world politics, fearful and cautious when evaluating, for example, peer politics. The mystery is why.

Why does the intellect operate unfettered and in full force on some topics, yet haltingly and self-consciously on others? A complete answer does not seem forthcoming. But, at least in my estimation, insight is gained when we look at the mental mechanisms which pull intelligence downward. The focus of this chapter – idea manipulation – will help us to better grasp some of the ways that adolescent intelligence undermines itself, especially in the adolescent's tendency to try to twist an idea to self-advantage.

Some Initial Observations Concerning the Adolescent's Mental Operations

One of the first things I try to impress upon anyone interested in learning about how adolescents think is that their thought is infused with nervous self-consciousness and fearful protectionism, both of which short-circuit the higher levels of their intelligence. These features of their phenomenology do not ruin their thought, but they seriously undercut its proficiency. Adolescents are *capable* of sophisticated reasoning, and, at the price of repeating myself, what adolescents are capable of and how they perform are two completely different realities. Adolescence is a time of tremendous disparity between potential and real, and part of the reason is that their intelligence is flooded with a self-consciousness which channels the thinking process into two directions, one dealing with the question at hand and the other dealing with the self and its nervous self-awareness of its own operations. This is not the only reason that adolescents have trouble thinking clearly and arguing evenly, but it is an important one.[1]

The disposition to be guided by the light of reason is not strong for most teens. This is not to say that they are predisposed to shade or conceal; rather, it is to say that nothing is built into their intellect which, on its own, impels them to search out the real, the genuine, the authentic. Every individual possesses a natural intelligence (which, of course, is not the same in every person), *but rigor and objectivity are not natural to intelligence* – they are acquired through imitation, through education, through coaching and coaxing. The acquisition of intellectual rigor (when it occurs) is one of the great advances of adolescence.

Intelligence, despite the great esteem in which it is held, is really not much without rigor and objectivity. Why? Because intelligence, without training, has no obligation to truth; the obligation of the intellect is to the self. Intelligence is not bound to reality, it is bound to its owner. For intelligence to be reality-bound, to be rigorous and disciplined, to be objective and impartial, it must be trained over a long period of time. Adolescence is the time when this training can optimally occur, and in North American culture, adolescence is when it is expected to occur.

Some youth watchers claim that to focus on the mental inefficiency of adolescents trivializes not only their thinking process, it trivializes them; I totally oppose this claim and I have actively fought against it in my career as an educator and as an author. The honest reporting of limitations never trivializes anything; but it does force us to reconsider many of our unexamined prejudices. Great nations, great leaders, great artists all have limitations and weaknesses, but this in no way implies they do not also have great strengths and admirable qualities. So it is with youth. At least that is how I see it.

At the risking of appearing apologetic about investigating these limitations of the adolescent thought process, I want to, once again, remind the reader that most adolescents possess tremendous intellectual potential, including the potential to think through propositions, to connect abstractions, to anticipate the future, and to double-check their own mental operations for errors. The "formal" thought which adolescents have at their avail is awesome in its speed and power; but even a Ferrari operates poorly if the cooling system isn't working properly.[2]

Idea Manipulation

The habits I describe in this section occur most frequently among eleven-fourteen-year-olds, but regardless of age, they come into play when teens are intellectually frustrated, emotionally uptight, or narcissistically threatened. Unfortunately, adolescents are intellectually frustrated, emotionally uptight and narcissistically threatened a great deal of the time, a fact which heightens their predisposition for inconsistent thinking, for unfair arguments, and for a host of other counter-productive thinking habits.

Adolescents, for the most part, are pragmatic in their thinking in that they typically are more concerned with outcomes and consequences than with procedure or protocol, and their arguments are governed by this pragmatic tone. Generally speaking, to which there are many exceptions, adolescents use arguments not as a way to tell right from wrong, but as a method of giving the voice of righteousness to their current thoughts.[3]

With these preliminary comments behind us, let us take a quick look at some of the idea manipulations teens employ to "win" their disputes.

(a) Making statements in which "all" is implied but "some" is true.

Arguing by universality when the question at hand is specific and local. "Everyone does it," when only some are doing it; "I'll be the only one who doesn't have one," when many do not. "Mr. Smith always picks on me," when Mr. Smith only once did so. This tendency is the product of either/or, right/wrong thinking so prevalent in the concrete thought of children, and the protectionist thinking of early adolescents.

> The tendency to over generalize makes it difficult to reason with adolescent girls. Because they know of one example, they'll argue "Everyone else gets to stay out till two," or "Everyone I know gets a new car for their sixteenth birthday." They'll believe that because the girl next door gets a ride to school, every girl in the universe gets a ride to school. They aren't being manipulative as much as they earnestly believe that one case represents the whole. (Pipher, 1996, p. 60)

(b) Using proof by selected instances.

"Jane's parents let her use their car and she never crashes it"; "Doing drugs doesn't hurt your grades: I have a friend who smokes pot and he's an honor student." The youngster who thinks, "I didn't make the team, I'm a real loser" is using proof by selected instances. So is one who argues: "Our principal has a tattoo and people respect *him*!." The advantage to this line of thinking is that it creates the illusion that one specific example of one real-life event is adequate grounds for justifying a larger issue. "If people like me don't get part-time jobs, how will the economy ever turn around?" This strategy is especially prevalent when youngsters are hard pressed to "prove" their point, or when they need a larger principle to confirm something specific to themselves.

(c) Opposing a proposition by misrepresenting it.

"I am opposed to kids having to do household chores and to all forms of child slavery." "I don't listen to feminists because they are lesbians."

A favorite misrepresentation is to disagree with what doesn't exist, or with what barely exists. "Abortionists hate babies, babies are our future." This strategy misrepresents an idea to better attack it. It most frequently occurs when the opposed idea is too strong to attack as it is; by misrepresenting and simplifying the idea, it becomes an easier target.

(d) **Diverting to a side issue when losing a point.**

"You always treat me like a kid." "You said I was old enough to make my own decisions," are examples of attacking the person rather than the issue in dispute. Arguing with her mother over whether she should be dating an older man, the daughter accuses: "At least I have a steady boyfriend. You go out with a different guy every week." All of this is in accord with the tendency to divert the the argument away from the main topic in order to gain the upper hand.

(e) **Promoting a conclusion simply because it is the mean between two extremes; claiming that compromise is always reasonable.**

Mother tells her daughter to be home at midnight; the daughter replies that she wants to return home at 4 a.m. An argument ensues. The child says: "OK, let's compromise, 2 o'clock." Notably missing from the reasoning process is that compromise involves more than merely halving the difference between two contested viewpoints. Enhancing one's position through compromise is even more appealing when it gives the impression of fairness.

(f) **Arguing so that no other conclusion is deemed plausible:** "Only an idiot would believe that disputes can be settled in the United Nations." "Every moral person knows that abortion is murder." Begging the question: "Why should I try to get people to like me; you can't be popular unless you're a cheerleader."

The extreme nature of these pronouncements is lessened by the adolescent tendency to perceive emotionally charged topics in black/white, all-or-nothing perspectives. This tendency is even more potent (hence, more resistant to reason) when the individual is frightened, defensive, or narcissistic.[4] At the risk of repeating myself, this means some youth all of the time, and all youth some of the time

(g) **Stating one's position over and over without defending the *merit* of the position.**

This involves the repetition of the same idea in different words, as if stating it over and over somehow makes it correct. "Tremaine quit school and he makes $50 000 a year." "Yah, but he's a drug dealer." "Yah, but he makes $50 000 a year." "He might get sent to prison, or get killed." "Yah, but he makes $50 000 a year." "Yah, but what he does is wrong." "Yah, but he makes $50 000 a year." Arguing in this way is an unwelcome exaggeration of the egocentric speech of childhood; it is grounded in the deception that the *act of saying* is as important as what actually is said.

This might be an appropriate time to introduce a parallel point. Adolescent arguing is often about scouting reactions *from one's own mind*. In other words, what one says is not necessarily an indicator of what one thinks as much as a sampling of idea fragments related to it. After numerous repetitions the target idea becomes progressively refined. Many so-called "arguments" are not arguments at all, but research into what one says when one is not certain what one thinks.

(h) **Failure to say exactly what it is that one is proposing.**

"School is stupid." "Teachers are unfair." "I'm tired of being exploited." Employing vagueness is helpful to the unfair agruer because it prevents the real topic from being investigated freely and openly. (In response to the parent's demand to know where the teen was until 2 a.m.: "Out." In response to what were you doing: "Nothing." In response to what do you hate about school: "Everything.") The refusal to use precise language protects one against a precise rebuttal, a fact of debate (and life) that most kids learn by grade six. In a heated argument it is not rare that neither opponent will make a clear, concise statement of any kind. These are not arguments in any real sense of that word, merely word-boxing.

(i) **Arguing by "straw-man."**

A "straw-man" argument is a bogus set-up knocked down to produce an easy victory. "Scientists make bombs because they don't care about the people they kill." "Straw-man" arguments are common fare for propagandists; their deception is in presenting points as logical when they are, in fact, artificial or false. It is an effective strategy with any audience which makes no effort to determine whether the point being knock down is relevant to the argument. (It is also effective with any group which simply enjoys seeing anything knocked down, no matter what it is).

"Straw-man" is similar to "red herring," a term which goes back to the seventeenth century when these strong-smelling fish were used by escaping criminals to cause bloodhounds to lose the human scent they had been following. This practice inspired the expression "to drag a red herring across the trail" which has been shortened to "red herring." Although adolescents may not know what a red herring is, they do know how to evade an issue by dragging in the irrelevant. "Straw-man" and "red herring" degrade discourse when they claim that which is important isn't and that which isn't is.

Why Manipulate Arguments?

But if thought can corrupt language, language can also corrupt thought.
(George Orwell)

In all of these strategies there is at work an elementary principle. You or I or an adolescent can honestly debate only when committed to *the actual points being debated.* This is precisely what ineffective arguers don't do. Instead of adjusting their mind to the issue, they adjust the issue to their needs and fears. The arguments which follow from these adjustments are bogus. What we have is not an argument, but the impersonation of an argument – an exchange where participants throw words at the argument's shadow. Shadow boxing. Encouragingly, in the intimacy of their reason, teens seem to recognize that these strategies are unfair, and, given the opportunity to see them for what they are, they are surprisingly willing to give them up for fairer ones. But getting them to see them for what they are is no small achievement, as any good high school teacher, or conscientious parent, will attest.

M. Piatelli-Palmarini makes some interesting observations on rationality in the human thought process, and this one is quite relevant to what I am trying to say about rationality (and clear thinking) during adolescence:

> Full-blown, self-checking rationality . . . does not act in us spontaneously or without effort. Rational judgment brings many different forces into play, and some of them are in conflict with each other. Rationality is not, therefore, even an immediate, psychological given; it is a complex exercise that is first won, and then maintained, at a certain psychological cost.(1994, p. 160)

Rationality is not given, it is won. Especially in the heat of an argument.

Rationality, whether exercised in problem-solving or arguments, can be practiced but it cannot be hurried. It takes the entirety of adolescence to cultivate an automatic, straight forward focus on the real object of intellectual investigation. During adolescence we learn to reason and we learn to argue, but, not quickly, nor on first try.

It is wrong to think of adolescents as intellectual contrarians, and please do not assume, even for a moment, that this is how I want to paint them. But to claim that their thinking is unbiased and unprejudiced is equally absurd. Like all of us, teens defend their ideas, but they have not as yet learned how to do it openly and honestly.[5]

The strategies which I have presented in the past few pages operate without much calculation or premeditation. They are, quite literally, part of the thought process itself, and this naturalness contributes immeasurably to the struggle with clear thinking and fair arguing. This particular point I do not want to get lost in the shuffle: the adolescent thought process devises its own means for idea manipulation. It may copy, or improvise on, manipulations seen elsewhere, but, it is fully capable of creating false inferences and manufacturing bogus arguments on the spot.

To be gleaned from all this is that idea manipulation is "natural" to the thought process, while objectivity and impartiality are learned, and learned slowly.

Reducing Idea Manipulation

> . . .it is valuable for adolescents to learn how to make informed, deliberate decisions rather than ignorant and impulsive ones. (David Hamburg)

What can we do to make better adolescent thinkers? This is a practical question to which many answers have been brought forward, some better than others, but none infallible. I find a good deal of common sense in an observation made by Raymond Nickerson: "It is not reasonable to expect that we shall discover any time soon how to turn our students into perfectly logical, consistent, thorough, sensitive thinkers. . . . What is reasonable to expect is a gradually better understanding of what it means to think well and how to promote good thinking" (1991, p. 7). To think well and to promote good thinking is the issue. But how to go about it?

A necessary starting point is to admit that adolescents are not *naturally* rational thinkers, which is to say that they are not by instinct, by hard-wire programming, by heredity, by predisposition, or by inclination completely rational beings. This is not to say that they are irrational, or anti-rational, even though some are; it is merely to say that clear thinking and systematic analysis are not *built into* their intellectual operations. Each of these valued traits is acquired, and while the acquisition process is easier for some than others, it is acquired. In the absence of the acquisition process, the adolescent thinker is bound to self-serving intelligence, with little concern for whether thought is rational or irrational. The adolescent's natural intelligence is one part utilitarian and one part narcissistic. To produce a thinker who thinks beyond these categories demands serious training.[7]

For those who prefer practical, "hands-on" suggestions on how to elevate the thinking of adolescents, I suggest the following as worthy starting points.

• Help teens to foster the habit of listening to what others have to say.

• Help teens to increase their willingness to consider points of view which differ from their own.

• Help teens to restrain their tendency to act impulsively.

• Help teens to use analogies effectively and appropriately.

• Help teens to objectively evaluate the merits of an argument.

• Help teens to recognize when peers are acting as narcissistic gratifiers, and when they are serving as objective evaluators.

• Help teens to recognize the difference between defending an idea and defending themselves; and, between criticizing an idea and criticizing the person who holds that idea.

• Help teens to recognize the differences between affective logic and impartial logic.

Final Comments

> We rarely find that people have good sense unless they agree with us. (de la Rochefoucauld)

In this chapter we have seen how adolescents bring the laws of their own nature into the rules of debate, creating problems for themselves and for debate. The conflict between these opposing forces can be resolved, and, in most instances, is. But the conflict can also linger, living into early adulthood and longer. Its legacy is an adult who argues like an adolescent; an unpleasant sight, but a common one, especially in dysfunctional families.

The purposes of arguments are many, and to discover the truth is only one. In this chapter I have detailed some of the ways that adolescents manipulate ideas in order to walk away from their arguments as "winners." Most of these manipulations have little to do with discovering the truth, and everything to do with appearing to have discovered it.

Anecdotes and Supplemental Information

[1]**Self-conscious emotions and the thinking process.** See *Self-conscious Emotions,* by J.P. Tangney and K. W. Fischer, Guilford Press, 1995, for a thorough overview of the self-conscious emotions and their influence on thought and behavior.

[2]**The need for critical thinking during early-adolescence** In the fairly recent past early adolescence was not a time of great concern as far as health and welfare were concerned because these youth rarely encountered situations where, if critical thought were briefly suspended, they would get into serious trouble. In today's world the story is completely different; drugs, automobiles, sexual behavior, weapons, gang warfare all place the young person at risk. For today's early-adolescent the temporary suspension of critical thought can spell the difference between a successful and a disastrous adolescent career.

[3]**The penchant for argumentation.** In the following passage Albert Schweitzer describes how his adolescent passion for arguing led him into all kinds of difficulties. In *Memories of Childhood and Youth,* he described his penchant for incessant argumentation.

> Between my fourteenth and sixteenth years I passed through an unpleasant phase of development, becoming an intolerable nuisance to everybody, especially to my father, through a passion for discussion. On everybody who met me in the street I wanted to inflict thorough-going and closely reasoned considerations on all the questions that were then being generally discussed, in order to expose the errors of the conventional views and get the correct view recognized and appreciated. . . . Thus I emerged from the shell of reserve in which I had hitherto concealed myself, and became the disturber of every conversation that was meant to be merely conversation. . . . If we went to pay a visit anywhere, I had to promise my father not to spoil the day for him by stupid behaviour during conversations. (Kiell, 1964, p. 482)

[4]**Awareness of good and bad arguments.** Teens are easily swayed by false arguments; not as easily as children, but more easily than adults. Most children, many teens, and few adults, for example, are tricked by what is known as ignoratio elenchi, a fallacy which supposes that an issue is proved or disproved by an argument which proves or disproves something else. An argument, for example, which demonstrates that the military is corrupt is used to "prove" that the family also is corrupt, is *ignoratio elenchi.*

[5]**The universal similarities in the adolescent experience.** Throughout this text I make reference to "North American youth." This is done to remind us that teen life here is not the same as everywhere else. However, I want to emphasize that in the technological countries of the world the similarities in teen life are profound. The emotional and intellectual composition of adolescents is essentially the same around the world. Differences between the youth of Canada and the United States, for example, are virtually non-existent. For that matter, the differences in adolescent life among any of the modern powers are slight. Teen-agers in Russia, France, Germany, Japan and Australia experience similar pleasures, disappointments, and frustrations because their biological needs, their intelligence, their future ambitions and their interpersonal tensions are very similar. Japanese boys worry about their unfolding body, their sexual attractiveness, and their social competence in ways difficult to distinguish from the manner in which the same topics are pondered by Russian girls. Youth in Ireland prepare for adult employment, matrimony, and a place to live, just as do the teen-age children of Ukrainian wheat croppers. That Northern Ireland is riddled with political strife and that Ukraine is encountering disfavour from Moscow are important political facts, but the problems of youth continue regardless of the problems of state. Samoan and Sicilian youth learn to live with their sexual passion; the fact that one society is rather permissive and the other rather restrictive toward expressing this passion is secondary to the fact that adolescent sexual passion exists and must be dealt with. Jewish parents encounter youthful rejection of tradition today just as they did in Czarist Russia because the intemperance of youth has always defied the caution of elders.

The universals of adolescence are as real as the universals of childhood.

[7]**A considerable element of practice is involved in presenting a reasoned argument.** Reason, like muscle, must be exercised, and arguments, like speech, must be rehearsed. To argue grossly, unfairly and narcissistically are inevitable first steps in the adolescent's journey to a more mature intellectual discourse.

Six

Why Adolescents Don't Think Clearly

The light of mature reason does not suddenly shed its clarity upon the young adolescent as by a magic wand. (E.A. Peel)

Virtually everything written on the topic of adolescent cognition speaks, in one way or another, to our chapter title. Several of the important themes have already been discussed, including the practical fact that teens are young and inexperienced with the rigors of formal thought, and that they are susceptible to a host of reasons-reducing peculiarities, including fables, illusions, and faulty arguments. This, of course, does not cover all of the possibilities.

Here I would like to leave some additional ideas which have not thus far been treated with sufficient care, the most notable being the adolescent fear of reason. The fear of reason does not exist as a conscious object-fear, such as the fear of heights or the fear of snakes where the person knows what he (she) is frightened of, but as a vague disquietude and a shaky resistance to giving one's mind over to calm, systematic thinking. Reason is the heart of critical thinking and adolescents fear it because, in the end, it may end up being critical of them. Reason opens the mind to new possibilities, but it can also expose inner ignorance. Reason makes no promises as to where it's going.

My comments in this chapter may be a bit too brief to withstand a healthy skepticism, so I present them as thought probes more than as anything else. Some of these ideas I have defended elsewhere, while others I am presenting here for the first time. At any rate, here are a few, worthy ideas about why adolescents have so much trouble thinking clearly.[1]

Why Youth Fear Reason

To conquer fear is the beginning of wisdom. (Bertrand Russell)

From a developmental view, adolescence is the time of life when the potential for reason transforms into its actualization. In no way is this transformation automatic or smooth. The process of becoming a reasoned thinker is slow, painful and pocked with intervals of backsliding regression. Many youth never complete the process, and for them reason is nothing more than a periodic visitor in their mental operations. Adolescents are neither inherently reasoning nor inherently reasonable.

Before youth are willing to commit to reason, they first must be convinced that something is in it for them; fortunately, this demand is easy to appease because the benefits to reason are abundantly clear to anyone with even a morsel of it. The practical allure of reason to the adolescent is that it offers the possibility of creating a correspondence between inner thought and the outer world, and the prospect of apprehending the world as it is. (A benefit, by the way, which holds no appeal to younger children because they do not as yet recognize that inner thought and outer world require integration.) Reason helps us to organize private experience into a mental scheme more coherent than experience itself, and it enables arguments to be cast into a demonstrative form, and therefore, to be better defended. Reason is attractive to youth because, when exercised properly, it is functional, productive, and self-serving. In all of these ways reason appeals to the practicality, common sense, and integrity of youth. But the *benefits* to reason are only part of the story.

For most teens reason is an unproven commodity, and therefore treated with caution. Adolescents know that reason is essential to knowledge and that to reason clearly is a virtue, yet they are apprehensive because they have no real mastery of it. The greatest obstacle to reason during adolescence is not the lack of it, but the fear of it. Fear puts frightening masks over the unknown, and reason, to the novice, is unknown.

Many factors conspire against reason during adolescence. The following, I believe, are among the more significant.

• Adolescents do not always know when reason merely reflects their prejudices, and when it is real and genuine. They are suspicious of reasoned conclusions because they don't know for sure when they are real and when they are bogus. Older, more experienced thinkers seem to use reason like a hammer to pound the argument of their opponents into submission. They come to resent reason and its unpredictable power.

To overcome their suspicion of reason adolescents need to see that reason works to their own ends, and more than anything, they need the guidance of someone who possesses more of it than they do.

• Reason does not inherently favor one idea over another; it is neutral. This neutrality stabs at the young person's desire to be favored. This competition between the impartial and the narcissistic is a profound struggle in adolescent development. Reason is feared because it can't be counted on as an emotional ally.

• Even-handedness, the very strength of reason, aggravates the young person's desire for priority. In a phrase, youth resent the *neutrality* of reason and the fairness of reason because they lessen self-priority. If you grasp this you will also see that youth fear reason because it robs them of their protective illusions. For all of these reasons adolescents are apprehensive and fearful about reason and the reasoning process.

• Teens fear that reason will convince them of what they don't want to be convinced of; and it often does. Since the outcome of reason is not predictable, it takes you where you don't always want to go. And who needs that? The persuasive power of reason is threatening to insecure thinkers.

• Creating a workable alliance between reason and emotion is one of the crowning achievements of adolescence, but, like so many advances during the second decade of life, it is several years in the making, and during those years we see periods when reason prevails and periods when emotion prevails. Adolescents fear that if reason ascends too rapidly, the richness of their emotional life will vanish, as if stolen by some force of calmness. This is the age when the philosophies opposed to reason first take hold. Cynicism, skepticism, nihilism, as well as the gentler rebellions of romanticism and naturalism, all appeal to the adolescent, in part, because of their defiance of reason and their exaltation of the mysterious, the untouchable unknowns of an unfathomable world. Young children have no need for protection from reason because they don't have enough of it to recognize its role in the world of thought.

• With increasing maturity reason attains a more forceful presence in the adolescent thinking process, but during *early* adolescence (twelve to fourteen) it easily recedes into the background of mental routine. Reason does not impose itself on the adolescent mind like some Guardian Angel of intelligence. Reason doesn't become "automatic" to mental operations until late-adolescence, and even then not completely.[2]

Amidst all this strife, an attitude of reason tries to take hold in the adolescent personality. By "an attitude of reason," I simply mean a mental posture where critical thinking is an entity in itself, where the object of thought is seen for what it is, not for how it is feared.

We are now brought to a realization which too few teachers and parents acknowledge: without reason intelligence is really quite pointless. Without reason intelligence has no direction, no way to explain or justify itself, no way to assess its own coherence, and no way to validate its own conclusions. Intelligence without direction is no small matter in the daily life of teens: it increases their at-risk behavior, narrows their moral outlook, and stymies meaningful self-analysis.

During adolescence reason is learned; reason is imitated; reason is acquired; reason is nurtured; reason is cultivated. But in no real sense is it natural or automatic. The adolescent thought process is fundamentally utilitarian and narcissistic, and not necessarily in that order. When reason is productive, useful, worthwhile it is learned quicker and with greater facility; when reason advances one's ambitions and when its conclusions flatter the self, it is learned quicker and with greater facility. This fact of adolescent intelligence holds profound implications for teachers and educators.

Narcissism

> When a man is wrapped up in himself he makes a pretty small package. (John Ruskin)

Adolescent intelligence is, in great measure, a narcissistic enterprise. By this I mean that at this stage of development the mind is driven more by self-serving than by truth-serving reflexes. It doesn't remain this way always; indeed much of the business of adolescent growth has to do with maturing beyond this kind of egocentric narrowness. But the adolescent's journey into expanded and enriched thought is impeded by an elementary ground rule: when intelligence is not trained outward to investigate the world on its terms, it deflects inwards to protect the self on its terms. Which is to say that when untrained to higher standards, the thought process remains narcissistic. In my assessment, this is the most profound phenomenon of adolescent intelligence.[3]

An example of the inward deflection to which I speak can be better understood by taking a look at a simple sentence. "That seems reasonable to me."

This sentence, simple and straightforward though it may appear, is completely different for thinkers dominated by an attitude of reason, and those by an attitude of narcissism. The key word in the sentence is different for each. To the reasoned thinker, (by which we mean the thinker in whom the thought process disciplines itself to focus on the evidence which supports, or does not support, an assertion) the key word is "reasonable." Implied is that a point has met the test of reason, common sense, or evidence. When the reasoned thinker says "That seems reasonable to me," he is making a statement about reasonableness, about coherence, about persuasiveness – the tools used to calculate truth or probable truth.

To the narcissistic thinker the sentence has a different meaning altogether; the key word shifts from "reasonable" to "me." To the narcissistic thinker (by which we mean the thinker in whom the thought process is accountable to needs and cravings rather than to reason or objectivity) the key word is "me." Implied is that a point, for whatever reasons, has been endorsed, validated, by "me." When the narcissistic thinker says "that seems reasonable to me," he is making a statement about "me," the decision-maker. Implied is the sovereignty of me, myself, not reason. This simple shift of emphasis changes the mood from objectivity to bias, from reason to egotism. It is no coincidence that it is a style of thinking favored by the fearful, the insecure, the uncertain, for under these emotional states the first obligation is to oneself.

Making "me" more important than reason is one of the benefits of narcissism, and every thinker, no matter at what age, thinks in this vein once in a while. But, at certain ages the predisposition to think narcissistically is stronger than at other ages. (During childhood and early-adolescence this tendency is at its peak.) Each individual is capable of different responses to this predisposition, and it is the response, not the predisposition, which determines whether reason or narcissism prevails. Those who are untrained to reason consistently prefer the narcissistic choice.

Narcissism is driven by brutally simple perceptions, the first of which is: "Does this help me or hurt me?" The barrenness of this starting point stifles the intellect by narrowing the focus to such a tiny point of self-concern that everything larger than the self is obliterated. (In fairness, we should point out that when the self and its immediate concerns are the object of one's thought – and they often are – then narcissistic narrowness can be a productive mental attitude. But when perspective is required, or seeing one's needs as only one among many is necessary, it is disastrous.) To advance intellectually adolescents must overcome the narcissistic bent within their thought process just as to advance intellectually children must overcome the egocentric bent within their thought process.

Here are a few ways that the narcissism of adolescence frustrates clear thinking.

• Narcissism inclines one to accept as true that which merely is flattering. Narcissistic thinkers are easily misled because of their predisposition to accept as true data which are not true at all. Formal thought (when it is operating at full capacity) monitors this predisposition and tries to hold it in check. When it succeeds the adolescent has taken a giant stride toward establishing reason and impartiality as dominant mental traits; when it fails, the adolescent has taken a giant stride toward the selfish intellectualism of "the narcissistic style." (See chapter nine for further elaboration of this concept.)

• Reason cannot exist as *an independent force* in a personality dominated by narcissism because narcissism demands favoritism in all matters Narcissism defies the first rule of reason: fairness.

• As is true for the egocentrism of childhood, the narcissism of adolescence shapes thought to its own ends without the thinker's awareness. Narcissistic intellectualism does not require conscious effort; in fact, the opposite: conscious effort is required to overcome the natural propensity to narcissism inherent to the thought process.

• Adolescents experience great confusion in distinguishing when their ideas are being attacked and when they themselves are being attacked. This confusion leads them to the erroneous belief that an attack on one *is the same as* an attack the other. The inability (or unwillingness) to distinguish an attack upon one's ideas from an attack upon one's person is a limitation teens share with children and with narcissists. As narcissism heightens, one is less able to distinguish an attack on "my" ideas from an attack on "me," conversely, as narcissism decreases, one is increasingly able to make this distinction. Consequently, it is impossible to debate fairly with individuals steeped in narcissism.

• Narcissistic thinkers accept as true that which affirms their importance, and as false that which negates their importance.

What then can we conclude about the role of narcissism in the adolescent thought process? First, adolescents are predisposed to self-serving, thought patterns, a predisposition which makes their first attempts at thinking through a particular problem biased and lacking in perspective. Second, narcissistic inclinations oppose calm reason, lowering the quality of adolescent thought. Third, adolescents must learn through practice, effort and training to reason their way through the narcissism natural to their thought process.

Are Adolescents Competent to Make Important Life Decisions?

This is a look at research which claims that adolescents are competent to make medical decisions affecting their own health.

An interesting piece of research conducted by Christopher Doig and Ellen Burgess (2000) at the University of Calgary's Department of Medicine raises some fundamental questions about the ability of adolescents to make fair and reasoned decisions about their own medical treatment. This research slices to the heart of what we are discussing in this chapter – the ability of the adolescent to think clearly about an emotionally charged topic. (As we noted in Chapter One, it is generally agreed that adolescents can think clearly when investigating a "neutral" topic not directly related to their emotional needs or to their vested interests.)

As a result of their research, Doig and Burgess concluded that adolescents are capable of making important health care decisions which directly affect their own lives, and, as well, that they are capable of making decisions concerning the withholding of their own life-sustaining treatment. The conclusions advanced in this study are important to physicians, psychologists, judges,and parents – indeed, all adults who hold a stake in the decision making of youth. They conclude their report with the following statement:

> Given that most adolescents have the capacity necessary to make competent health care decisions, the ethical physician should respect this and allow the competent adolescent the right to exercise autonomy. (p. 1587)

In other words: since adolescents are able to competently make these decisions, they should be allowed to do so. This conclusion adds controversy to legal decisions previously rendered on this topic. For example, in 1979 Justice

Warren Burger, of the U.S. Supreme Court, wrote the following judgment on adolescent mental competence.

> The law's concept of the family rests on a presumption that parents possess what a child lacks in maturity, experience, and capacity for judgment required for making life's difficult decisions. *Most children, even in adolescence, simply are not able to make sound judgments concerning many decisions, including their need for medical care or treatment.*

In this passage, Justice Burger's viewpoint is clearly aligned with the prevailing themes of this text, namely, that adolescents lack mental maturity and life experience, and, as a result, they *are less inclined to* (not the same as "not able to") make decisions calmly, rationally, and effectively. Burger's ruling, on the face of it, seems to contradict the findings of Doig and Burgess. However, Burger's ruling is not the only one on this topic.

In 1972, Justice William Douglas, also of the U.S. Supreme Court, wrote: "The moral and intellectual maturity of the fourteen-year-old approaches that of the adult." Here we have what appears to be two conflicting views on the mental competence of adolescents. Justice Burger and Justice Douglas succinctly summarize the opposing opinions on whether adolescents have the ability to make critical health care decisions.

The authors of the University of Calgary study report that adolescents ". . . have the capacity necessary to make competent health care decisions." But, it seems to me, this "capacity" is not nearly as well developed as Doig & Burgess imply. For example, before important health care decisions can be made, the adolescent must receive explicit medical information and numerous visits with the supervising clinician. According to the authors: "Sincere attempts to communicate this information must be made even if this requires numerous clinical visits. The physician should assess an adolescent's ability to comprehend and reflect on the choices, to balance values, and to understand the implications of treatment decisions."

In essence, these researchers are saying that:

• when the adolescent has all relevant information carefully presented, and

• when the attending physician has fully explained the meaning of this information, and

• when the physician has assessed the adolescent's ability to comprehend what has been explained, and

• when the physician has ascertained that the adolescent understands the implications of his (her) decision,

then the adolescent is competent to render an appropriate decision. When one looks closely at these particular findings it can be seen that the "competence" of the adolescent decision-maker is, in great measure, a function of the competence of the attending physician.

These "qualifications" on adolescent thinking are exactly what I have been trying to convey. The adolescent has the *potential* to make tough decisions, the ability to analyze complex variables, and the *capacity* to step outside of oneself to take in the larger picture. However, this potential, this ability, and this capacity are not actualized spontaneously; in order to work efficiently they require mentoring, guidance, and training. Since all of these conditions were met in their particular research setting, it is not surprising that the authors found that adolescents were capable of solid decision-making.

Yet, the prickly question remains. Can adolescents think clearly enough to be consistently competent decision makers? The answer depends on the circumstances. When an effort is made to provide the adolescent with solid evidence, to ensure that the adolescent thinks calmly, to encourage the adolescent to take the necessary time for a thorough analysis of the problem, *then*, "Yes."

On the other hand, when adolescents must make decisions outside these ideal circumstances, the outlook is not nearly so encouraging. This is no small matter, because in our society the gravest decisions facing youth occur in hurried situations charged by peer pressure, sexual arousal, anger; further, these decisions often concern issues about which the adolescent has very little first hand experience. These are not at all "ideal conditions" for competent decision making. Under these hurried and emotional conditions, "No."

, So, at the end we are back to the beginning. Adolescents have tremendous *potential* for decision-making, but this potential does not come into maturity on its own. As A.E. Peel, the renowned psychologist, put it: "The light of mature reason does not suddenly shed its clarity upon the young adolescent as by a magic wand." Effective decision-making requires solid information, time to think, a good mentor, and, lots of practice. When these conditions are met, the higher reaches of adolescent intelligence take hold of the thinking process and "the sky is the limit." When these conditions are not met (and usually they are not) adolescent decision-making is much more hit-and-miss because teens often fear the reasoning process, and they prefer a narcissistic choice when one is available.

Final Comments

Reason is that by which the soul thinks and judges. (Aristotle)

I seek nothing more than to encourage clarity and honesty about a topic which, at this moment in our understanding, has little of either. I feel a bit like what the psychologists of the 1920s and 1930s must have felt when they tried to describe the intelligence of children in terms of what it actually could or could not do, rather than in terms of what the popular wisdom of that time demanded it should be able to do.

The popular wisdom of our era ascribes to *adolescents* a rationality they do not possess. It is my belief, and one which I hope that I have well demonstrated, that the adolescent thought process, by the nature of its internal operations, is *prone toward* irrationality, and *prone toward* error. The vast reserves of reason which bless adolescent intelligence do not take hold on their own; they must be nurtured, cultivated and practiced repeatedly if they are to work effectively. An attitude of reason is neither natural nor automatic; it is learned and it is earned. These facts of the adolescent's mental ecology impose upon adults a more profound responsibility for nurturing the adolescent thought process than any of the current experts has heretofore acknowledged.[4]

We can find nothing in the thought process which, on its own, pushes youth to think systematically or clearly. Adolescent thought, like the thought of children, must be nurtured and coached beyond its natural boundaries, and, as well beyond the vision it holds for itself and its possibilities.

Adolescents are genetically designed to think, but not to think clearly. This they must learn; if they don't they won't.

Anecdotes and Supplemental Information

[1]**Clear thinking, beclouded thinking, and why teens don't think clearly.** The squandering of intellectual capacity is one of the great mysteries of adolescent psychology. *Beclouded thinking* is the tendency for thought to become hazy, foggy, blurred, inconsistent, self-serving, and, most usually, inaccurate; it is not complete brain meltdown, but thinking at reduced efficiency.

Critical thinking is neutrally reasoned evaluation which requires one to categorize, infer, and deduce. Critical thinkers must, of course, know something about the content in question; for example, to evaluate a reformer's ideas about changing the school system, one must be knowledgeable about the existing school system. Critical thinking, then, relies on having substantive knowledge about the topic to which thought is directed.

But this is not all. A critical thinker must also have solid knowledge about how his or her own thinking process works: "Effective critical thinking requires a person to monitor when she really understands an idea, know when she needs new information, and predict how easily she can gather and learn that information" (Seifert & Hoffnung, 1994, p. 532). Critical thinkers must possess some criteria of fairness and objectivity, and enough insight into their own mental operations to know when they are straying from fairness and objectivity. Critical thinking involves skillful judgment as to truth and merit.

[2]**The early adolescent as thinker**. Early adolescents, when compared with late adolescents, do not comprehend well the social forces of history, nor do they have much insight into the causes of international power struggles. Unflatteringly, their understanding of society and its internal machinery seems to be based as much on platitudes and pledges as on genuine insight. Their sense of social purpose tends to be based as much on authority as on justice.

Early adolescents are *easy* to teach because they believe in the power of authority, because their thought assimilates more easily than it accommodates, and because they possess limited ability to disagree with ideas too removed from their own experience. They are difficult to teach because they think they know more than they do, because they question better than they understand, and because their powers of induction are weakened by lack of experience in the real world and their powers of inference are impeded by cognitive immaturity.

All in all, early adolescents are not naturally cooperative, but cooperation is easily learned; they are capable of genuine sharing, but equally capable of genuine selfishness. They enjoy doing the right thing, but they require specific instruction before they can recognize it.

[3]**Narcissism and faulty thinking.** To encourage new perceptions about the adolescent experience, I am here suggesting that some of the core concepts of narcissism, seen in the proper light, can help us to better understand why adolescents have trouble thinking clearly.

I have embarked on this venture because it seems to me that we have not made much progress in understanding why adolescents so easily choose self-destructive paths. It is not an exaggeration to say that we simply do not understand why they so easily become involved in relationships destructive to their emotional, economic, and human welfare. We have a long journey to travel before we understand why teens, as Judith Musick phrased it, "turn their back on opportunities, deliberately sabotaging their prospects for success" (1993, p. 4).

What we need, and cannot lay our finger on, is a worthy explanation as to why some adolescents think clearly enough to avoid self-destructive choices while others, with similar thinking skills, do not. Hopefully, our investigation will shed some light on this mystery.

[4]**Adolescent thought encounters periods of intellectual regression.** Adolescence is an era of transition, but these transitions do not flow in smooth progressions, but in clutches and spurts. One outcome of this crab-like cadence is that teens, every now and again, regress to thought modes which worked effectively in childhood but which cannot handle the complex demands of adolescence. Cognitive psychologists refer to this intellectual slippage as "regression to concrete thought." As we recall from materials introduced in earlier chapters, at the "concrete" level of intellectual development children sometimes accept hypotheses as facts and they sometimes reject facts as if they were mere hypotheses. This failure to differentiate "actual facts" from "mere hypotheses" fogs the thought process considerably.

Rarely does it occur to young children to re-evaluate a belief simply because evidence does not support it. Children believe that because the hypothesis is "mine" it holds a special validity, that it is imbued with its own logical consistency; therefore, it does not seem reasonable to them to change a belief when new information contradicts it.

Among mature thinkers, when evidence fails to support a hypothesis, it is re-examined on the chance that something was missed. Children almost never follow this procedure. Thus, an eleven-year-old who believes that he is the best baseball player in the 5th grade, and predicts that he will be the first player chosen when teams are selected, may not alter his belief even when he is chosen last. He may simply interpret the facts in a self-enhancing way, i.e., "The other players are jealous of me," "I really didn't want to play on this team." The point here is that the belief is not rejected simply because it is not supported.

Adolescents, much more than children, face evidence when and where it presents itself and, as a result, they re-work and re-shape their beliefs in the light of new evidence. "Maybe the coach is right. I'm not as good as I thought." Nothing heroic here, simply modifying a belief to fit the data; a normal indicator of maturing thought.

Section Two

Selfishness and Togetherness

Seven

The Natural Selfishness of Youth

Adolescence is a time of intensely heightened narcissism and self-pre-occupation. (D.B. Wexler)

In the vast literature of adolescent psychology, almost nothing has been written about selfishness. Consequently, here in the first decade of the 21st century, we are chronically uninformed on this topic. While everyone seems aware that selfishness, in one form or another, is a defining trademark of youth, we have not gone very far toward understanding its psychological dimension. The word itself conjures hostile images and fearful connotations. When we describe adolescents as "selfish," it is hard to create a sympathetic attitude. We have no choice except to put this discomfort aside if we want to create anything which resembles a unified field theory of adolescent behaviour; there is no understanding of youth when there is no understanding of the selfishness which spices it.

One reason we know so little about the legitimate and natural expressions of selfishness is that Sigmund Freud, and his daughter, Anna Freud, whose ideas shaped the early and middle decades of 20th century psychology, viewed adolescent selfishness as merely one variation on the primal, hostile selfishness which tarred human nature; they saw adolescent selfishness as mere spillage from the libidinal cauldron which motivates all human behavior. This Freudian view of selfishness created a suspiciousness toward every expression of selfishness, including the gentler egotism natural to adolescence. Our understanding of natural selfishness is not nearly so bleak; indeed, it is not bleak at all.[1]

My initial assumption on this topic is that selfishness shows itself in both healthy and unhealthy ways, and in this, the first of three chapters on the topic of adolescent selfishness, I will try to explain something of its healthy side.

I adhere to the view that the inclination to self-priority and self-immersion is fundamental to children and adolescents, and would also be to adults except for the fact that cooperative living and civil life cannot exist when these traits monopolize one's consciousness. Neither can one raise children and train them to altruistic habits when one is perpetually self-absorbed and self-possessed.

Developmental selfishness is as natural to adolescents as egocentrism is to children; like egocentrism, it shrouds their character with a pressing egoism and a nervous, invigorating, self-awareness. Developmental selfishness is not the greedy, fearful, and protectionistic selfishness that we see in pathological selfishness (the focus of the next chapter). Rather, it is a normal, natural and inevitable fact of adolescent development. Thus, we have arrived at our starting point – certain expressions of selfishness are normal, even healthy.

Developmental Selfishness as a Natural and Normal Condition of Youth

> The ego needs to be loved, requires attention, and wants exposure. That is part of its nature. (Thomas Moore)

Thomas Moore sets the stage nicely because our first message is that every person wants love, attention and recognition. These cravings are natural, and from them grows the desire to be the object of attention, to receive admiration, and to be flattered. The extent to which these cravings dominate the personality greatly determines the destiny of the adolescent personality. For the moment our concern is with the "naturalness" of the ego's need to be loved and made the object of affection, and with the "natural" and "legitimate" self-centredness that comes with it. That is, with the natural selfishness of youth.

The preliminary groundwork for understanding developmental selfishness is straightforward: adolescents are infused with a normal and developmentally driven self-ish-ness which, while not as innocent as that which graces children, *is equally grounded in their particular stage of life*. Developmental selfishness, as I am here describing it, involves the persistent experience of one's own feelings, fears, and desires, and the emotional self-conscious charge which comes with that experience. This persistent, emotionally-charged awareness causes the adolescent to perceive almost everything within the context of self. This natural selfishness is the embodiment of the vital force and animated character which describes healthy youth.

We want to learn more about it because it is natural, because it is universal, and because under the right conditions it matures into adult self-confidence, and under the wrong conditions it erodes into unhealthy, overbearing, narcissistic selfishness.

Let's begin by refreshing our understanding of egocentrism, because it is the heart and soul of natural selfishness. To be egocentric is to be preoccupied with one's own concerns and insensitive to the concerns of others. Piaget understood it as an *embeddedness* in one's own point of view, in one's own perceptions, and in one's own emotions. Very young children cannot distinguish their own point of view from the point of view of others; they may not even know what "a point of view" is. Most developmentalists assume that young children (toddlers and preschoolers) do not seem to know that other perceptions of reality exist, but older children and adolescents do. And this is one of the differences between children and adolescents – the awareness of alternate viewpoints. Margaret Donaldson put it this way: "the child does not appreciate that what he sees is relative to his own position; he takes it to represent absolute truth or reality – the world as it really is" (1978, p. 20). Developmentalists agree that the egocentrism of children is more powerful and more pervasive than the egocentrism of adolescents; nevertheless, egocentrism is a forceful presence in the mental lives of all teens. *The natural egocentrism of childhood is the phenomenological starting point for the developmental selfishness of adolescence.*

Developmental selfishness fosters a preoccupation with, and a heightened sensitivity to, everything that pertains to "me:" not only the positive, i.e., that which praises, validates, or affirms "me," but also with the negative, i.e., that which criticizes, weakens or deflates "me." This incessant preoccupation with self heats the vanity and the oratory of youth, igniting an attentiveness to everything touching the majesty of the self. This is the natural selfishness of youth, a solipsism of the present moment, an extreme concern with, and hyper-responsiveness to, the self and everything in its orbit.[2]

That youth are selfishly preoccupied and wrapped up in themselves is certainly not a new observation. Aristotle, the most meticulous and methodical of the early observers, felt the lava in the blood of Athenian youth, and he said as much when documenting their habits and inclinations:

> They are passionate, irascible, and apt to be carried away by their impulses. They are the slave, too, of their passion, as their ambition prevents their ever brooking a slight and renders them indignant at the mere idea of enduring an injury. . . . If the young commit a fault, it is always *on the side of excess and exaggeration* for they carry everything too far, whether it be their love or hatred or anything else. (Kiell, 1964, p. 18-19)

While it is likely that Aristotle exaggerated both the virtues and the defects of youth, there is little reason to doubt that some basis in fact existed for his observations. Indeed, when he reported that youth were self-centred and "selfish" in 300 B.C., there is every reason to believe that he reported accurately. (No historical author, to my knowledge, has ever reported that the youth of that era were lacking in the qualities we are here describing). Anna Freud, 2300 years after Aristotle, judged that North American teens ". . . are excessively egoistic, regarding themselves as the centre of the universe and the sole objects of interest." Both Aristotle and Anna Freud, despite their over-statement, were, in their own way, trying to tell us about the self-centredness, the self-priority, indeed, the selfishness, natural to youth.[3]

I am here trying to convey a simple idea: adolescents possess a vigilant spirit which invigorates their sense of themselves and creates within them a sustained egoism. This "sustained egoism" colors their perceptions of the world, it narrows their vision, and its makes them more alive to the realities within their boundaries than to those outside it. The end result is an uneven concoction of self-love, self-centredness, and selfishness, leading Gordon Allport, one of North America's great psychologists, to conclude: "Self-love may be prominent in our natures without necessarily being sovereign." And that pretty much sums it up: selfishness is prominent in the adolescent's nature without being sovereign. All young people do not experience it with identical intensity, or express it with identical vigor, but all healthy youth possess it in rich supply.

The parallel between the egocentrism of children and the selfishness of adolescence is an interesting one, and certainly worth a moment of our time. To mature emotionally and intellectually children must learn to test their own perspectives and points of view against those of others, and they must acquire the ability to inspect their own inferences and conclusions for accuracy and validity. This process is a slow and methodical one, with gradual increments occurring annually throughout childhood. By age nine, or ten, or eleven, most youngsters are shedding the cloak of egocentrism which warms and shelters their unfolding self. This does not mean they are no longer egocentric, as no one is completely without egocentrism; rather, that they can take a posture in regard to their own egocentrism, inspect it, review it, and place it under their own mental microscope. From all these age-driven advances their egocentrism becomes a less imposing fact of their personality. Instead of dominating their perceptions and judgments, it assumes a more secondary status in the phenomenology of everyday life. This is why we say that Maria seems more mature, more composed, and more aware of her surroundings as an eleven-year-old than she did a year ago as a ten-year-old. Egocentrism, in general, weakens with each advancing year during childhood, and from this gradual weakening the personality gradually strengthens.

The natural selfishness of adolescence follows a similar path. The self-entrenchment and wholesome imperviousness which defines developmental selfishness lessens throughout the course of adolescence. The nonchalant indifference to the outside world is challenged by the growing capacity to see the world through eyes other than one's own, and, of course, by the blunt realism of the world itself. The juvenile propensity to condense the world into the microcosm of one's own interests and involvements simply cannot handle the demands we place on late-adolescents and young adults in our culture. So, inevitably, the developmental selfishness of youth, like the egocentrism of childhood, weakens in order to accommodate increased responsibility and expectation.

Developmental Selfishness as Healthy Narcissism

> What renders the vanity of others insupportable is that it wounds our own. (de la Rochefoucauld)

In psychological literature, the positive side of narcissism is known as "healthy narcissism," "productive narcissism," or "favorable narcissism." Harold Barrett, for example, writes, "Favorable narcissism mobilizes behavior to beneficial purposes and is represented by normal self-concern and an adequate level of self-esteem: productive pride, we might call it" (1991, p. 34). He then adds: "The mighty engine that drives the self in all interaction is abetted by the individual's inimitable stock of narcissistic energy. . ." (p. 64). Narcissism's healthy side inspired Carl Goldberg to write: "I view *healthy* narcissism as enhancing to the fulfillment of human existence. . . . Narcissistic strivings coexist with mature object love, both confounding and enriching its development. . . Narcissism, in its positive sense, is an enrichment of human experience" (1983, p. 13).

As far as adolescents are concerned, this makes sense. After all, a vibrant self-concept without some narcissism is really quite unthinkable. What person could honorably exist without self-love and self-admiration? We all are characterized by a selfish core which is a vital, worthy part of our being. Erich Fromm, one of the first Neo-Freudians to envision the tremendous implications of the theory of narcissism, claimed: "Even in the average individual . . . there remains a narcissistic core which appears to be almost indestructible." Further, "in the case of normal development, man remains to some extent narcissistic throughout his life." Finally, and perhaps most significantly: "We can say that nature had to endow man with a great amount of narcissism to enable him to do what is necessary for survival" (all quotes taken from Fromm's landmark essay, "Individual and Social Narcissism").

Positive narcissism is an important side of the "selfishness" story; it helps us to better understand the "I'm-glad-I-am-me" vitality of youth. Whether we call it "positive narcissism" or "developmental selfishness," what we are getting at is primal assertion heated by self-righteousness.

The selfishness I am here clumsily describing is not grounded in a hostile disregard for others, nor in pushing one's own advantage at the expense of others; it is a friendly, natural self-centredness which does not need to degrade others in order to bolster itself. It is its own reward, its own validation, and so natural that many teens, especially the younger ones, don't know, in any abstract way, even that they possess it. The natural selfishness of youth is spiced with vanity and self-reference – but it is not based on a sense of superiority, or an attitude of condescension. Think of it as egocentric embeddedness in an outwardly propelled self, a state of mind where self-awareness and self-arousal are constantly operating at full capacity; where the mind is perpetually bombarded by the rush and excitement of self awareness. The natural selfishness of youth is an aliveness to life's possibilities as they relate to one's self, one's feelings, and one's understanding of life.

When we talk about developmental selfishness we are talking about the vitality, the arrogance, the charm of youth. When we love youth we love the developmental selfishness inherent to it. When properly acknowledged and lovingly nourished it grows into altruism, social interest, reciprocity and mutuality. On its own it is none of these things; but when nurtured, this is what it becomes. Developmental selfishness, as far as human growth and development is concerned, is not an end in itself. Like the egocentrism of childhood, it must grow beyond itself to become more than it is.

The underlying theme to chapters Seven, Eight, and Nine is that different expressions of selfishness are associated with different levels of psychological health. Although we are early in the development of this theme, a chart outlining its general points is seen on this page. In a nutshell, it is here claimed that developmental selfishness is part of the adolescent's normal psychological functioning, and natural to the phenomenology of youth.When development proceeds on schedule, the natural selfishness of youth matures into the healthy egotism of adulthood. When development does not proceed on schedule, when it is thwarted, when it lacks mentoring, when the adolescent does not invest in others or share in their concerns, developmental selfishness may erode into an unhealthy self-obsession which results, most typically, in a condition of borderline dysfunction I call "the narcissistic style."

Psychological Health and Selfishness

This chart helps us to envision the relationship between selfishness and psychological health. The top line indicates the continuum of psychological health ranging from normal psychological functioning through psychiatric disorder, i.e., from healthy to unhealthy. The bottom line represents the continuum of selfishness, ranging from normal developmental selfishness through pathological selfishness, i.e., from healthy to unhealthy. The categories on each continuum match those directly above (or below).

Psychological Health

Normal psychological functioning ..... Borderline disorder.........Psychiatric disorder

Selfishness

Developmental Selfishness ....The Narcissistic Style............Pathological Selfishness

All selfishness, quite obviously, is not natural and healthy. The emotionally diminishing and socially debilitating expressions of selfishness are the focus of the next two chapters.

Anecdotes and Supplemental Information

[1] **Freud's understanding of narcissism.** Freud understood narcissism as the turning of love away from the world and inward upon the self, making the self the object of its own investment. Freud also believed that every person begins life in a blissful state of "primary narcissism" where no distinction exists between self and world; this is a stage of development where the infant has not as yet established any ego boundaries, and thus experiences itself and its environment as one. Primary narcissism bestows the child with feelings of perfection and power, wholeness and harmony. This is a blissful fusion so profound that youth spend their adolescent years trying to recapture at least part of its self-aggrandizing glory.

Freud also believed that primary narcissism is the stage of psychosexual development, where the child's pleasures are concentrated within the self and the body; a developmental stage when autoerotic sensations become fused into one's body, which then become a single, unified love object. This "narcissistic condition" is the libidinal storehouse from which not only love of self, but love in general, emerges.

Eventually, much of the child's primary narcissism is abandoned in favor of ego development, and in time, the child replaces self-love with love for others. *But the love received from others cannot equal the primal glory of self-love.* In narcissistic theory, this final point is vital, as it claims self-love is more powerful, indeed more basic, than the love of others. The acceptance or rejection of this starting point greatly shapes how we view adolescent love.

[2] **Historical context for "developmental selfishness."** That adolescents are consumed with the demands of their own development is the starting point of modern adolescent theory. The term that I am using here, "developmental selfishness," is new, but the fire behind it was felt by all contributors to adolescent theory. Erik Erikson's concept of psychosocial stages; Anna Freud's theory of psychosexual development; Peter Blos' second individuation process; Jean Piaget's theory of adolescent egocentrism; David Elkind's personal fable; Robert Havighurst's developmental tasks; Arnold Gessel's reciprocal interweaving; and Robert Selman's theory of perspective-taking each, in their own way, speak to the proposition that adolescence is a period of life when the individual is consumed by a necessary, and legitimate, self-investment, self-centredness, self-ish-ness.

[3] **Aristotle and Anna Freud.** An important difference between Aristotle and Anna Freud on this topic is that Freud's understanding of youth was shaped by her assumption that libidinal selfishness (the id) was the fundamental motivation to human behavior; when she described the selfishness of youth, her observations completely supported her premises. Aristotle, on the other hand, had no organized theory of adolescent behavior, he simply described what he saw. That their accounts of youth are similar is, however, an interesting testimony to the constancy of the attitudes, behaviour and temperament of youth.

Eight

Pathological Selfishness

Although an accentuated self-awareness is a normal part of adolescence, *excessive selfishness* is dysfunctional . . . (Lauren Ayers)

We began our investigation in the previous chapter by describing the normal and natural selfishness of youth which I call "developmental selfishness." In the way I am viewing it, developmental selfishness refers to the natural egotism and legitimate self-centredness of childhood and adolescence. The term carries neither psychiatric nor moral overtones. The focus here in this chapter, however, is with an expression of selfishness more extreme and more pathological than anything found in normal developmental selfishness.

The most pathological form of self-centredness could be called "narcissistic selfishness." I am introducing it in this chapter for two reasons. The first is to show the extremes to which selfishness can evolve in the human personality; the second to show how the beginnings of this outrageous selfishness begin to flower during adolescence. I am not suggesting that narcissistic selfishness is a fact of adolescence; it isn't. Rather, I am trying to set the stage for a look at the subdued form of narcissistic selfishness, called "the narcissistic style," which during adolescence expresses itself as entitlement-driven self-priority.

The quote from Lauren Ayers at the top of the page is an important one which we will draw upon many times in the immediate chapters. With selfishness, as with all psychiatric conditions, *degree* is everything. As has already been established, a normal degree of selfishness lives in the heart of every healthy person. Without it, survival is impossible in our culture – perhaps in every culture. However, as Ayers rightly observes, excessive selfishness not only becomes dysfunctional to the individual, but also to the group which nurtures and supports the individual. Narcissistic selfishness is not only a psychiatric disorder, it is a social and moral catastrophe. Once again, to set things straight, this disorder is not common in the adolescent community. But its reduced version, the narcissistic style, the subject of the next chapter, is.

The Extremes of Human Selfishness

> The most unambiguous sign that one holds men in contempt is this, that one
> acknowledges them only as a means to *one's own* ends or does not acknowl-
> edge them at all. (Friedrich Nietzsche)

In ordinary language, narcissism refers to vanity, illusory love, and chronic self-absorption, and an infatuation with self so extreme that the interests of
others are ignored. Narcissism represents a turning of love away from the
world and inward upon the self. Hence, the narcissistic self is obsessed with
its own gratification, but in addition, is burdened with a morbid fear of humiliation and an unhealthy fear of losing. In order to make clear how narcissistic
selfishness differs from other expressions of selfishness, let me describe it in
some detail.

Narcissistically selfish persons are always anxiously concerned with
themselves and obsessively immersed in their own immediacy; they are rest-
less, and driven by the fear that they will not get enough of whatever it is that
they want. This free-floating fear completely dulls the pleasure they receive
when they do attain what they crave. Important to their friendship patterns,
they do not experience much pleasure when they *give*, but they experience
pleasure when they receive. They lack compassion, they have almost no genuine mercy, and they show little concern for the needs of others; they judge
everyone from the standpoint of their usefulness in satisfying "my" needs and
"my" desires.[1]

Despite their over-whelming sense of self-priority, these individuals are
not social isolates, or even loners, because they cannot maintain any sense of
themselves without massive infusions of attention and admiration from the
very people for which they hold no genuine fondness. Their social life
becomes a massive quest for admiration and respect. When they do not
receive it they are resentful, hateful and aggressive. (Nothing is more frightening than a frustrated narcissist who has access to a deadly weapon.)

One of the paradoxes of narcissistically selfish people is that even though
they do not much care for other people in their own right, they are, at the same
time, completely dependent on others to provide the attention and admiration
without which they will disintegrate. Thus, while fundamentally selfish, they
cannot live a hermit's life; they desperately need others *as providers*. Their
ravenous hunger for attention and admiration drives them to solicit the acceptance, the recognition, and the love which confirms their worth. Even though
they hold no empathetic bond with their companions, their family, their loved
ones, they have a complete dependency on them for the emotional nourish-
ment they provide. This dependency, like clockwork, turns into resentment
and hostility, creating the love-hate relationships for which the narcissistically
selfish are universally known.

Their obsession with grooming, with physical appearance, and with presenting a beautiful body, rather than building confidence within them, triggers a chronic envy of these features in others. They crave and hate the same thing at the same time: they love stylish haircuts when they have one, but hate them when they are "flaunted" by someone else; they love to walk with confidence, but hate the cocky swagger of those who walk the walk; they love to be the object of admiration, but despise the admiration given to others, even their loved ones.

Envy is a prevailing mood state of the narcissistically selfish. This burdensome envy causes them to perceive others in terms of their own yearnings and desires, and to project their insecurities onto them. Envy characterizes all of us to some degree, but among the narcissistically selfish it is relentless, percolating hostility toward any competitor who receives praise or glory. (This, by the way, helps us to understand why narcissistically selfish individuals are so spiteful toward those who receive praise and promotion.) Nancy McWilliams explains it this way:

> Envy may also be the root of the much-observed judgmental quality of narcissistically organized persons, toward themselves and toward others. If I feel deficient and I perceive you as having it all, I may try to destroy what you have by deploring, scorning, or criticizing it (1994, p. 172).

Narcissistically selfish individuals cannot handle relationships in which give and take exist in equal portions; therefore, basic needs which require equality for their gratification (intimacy, deep friendship) are never satisfied. Their relationships become quagmired in empty investments; they displace their feelings of unworthiness onto others, and their contempt for themselves becomes contempt for others, even their friends, their parents, and their lovers. Narcissists hold everyone in contempt because, at bottom, they hold themselves in contempt.[3]

Narcissistically selfish individuals seek relationships where they are perpetually praised but never challenged; this is what they seek in friendship – praise without criticism. Finding companions to serve this function is their social mission; without "suppliers" (who they call "friends,") they have no purpose, no meaning, no direction. Hence, narcissists are always on the recruitment trail, always in search of friends who will provide them with their needed emotional supplies.

> It is definitely a two person relationship in which, however, only one of the partners matters; his wishes and needs are the only ones that count and must be attended to; the other partner, though felt to be immensely powerful, matters only insofar as he is willing to gratify the first partner's needs and desires or decides to frustrate them; beyond this, his personal interests, needs, desires, wishes, etc., simply do not exist. (Nelson, p. 104)

On occasion the selfish nature of these individuals is confused with high self-esteem. Indeed, this is one of the more common rationalizations among those they have cultivated as friends. "He isn't really selfish, he is just extremely confident." "He doesn't disrespect others, he is just so wrapped up in the demands of his own world that he cannot tolerate weakness in others." This is not so. Narcissism and self-esteem are two completely different forms of self-awareness, totally different in dynamics and expression. High self-esteem has nothing to do with praise-crazy self-priority. Positive self-esteem doesn't mean "I'm OK, you're irrelevant." Self-esteem is not self-inflation; narcissists accept self-inflation wherever they find it, individuals with high self-esteem accept honest, fair praise. Self-esteem means trusting yourself, being competent to cope with life challenges. Individuals with positive self-esteem are not enraged when someone points out a flaw in their character. Narcissists, in the solitude of their soul, are too frightened of love and life to possess genuine self-esteem. (An interesting aside to this issue is that most adolescents are not very skilled at recognizing the difference between genuine self-esteem and narcissistic bravado. This limitation within their character, which derives from a lack of experience in motive analysis, exposes their vulnerability to every form of fakery and charlatanism.) [4]

.   .   .

Here we have taken a brief, essentially clinical, look at the toxic lifestyle known variously as "pathological selfishness," or "narcissistic selfishness." I am not trying to make the case that narcissistic selfishness is universal in the adolescent community, because it is not. However, its weaker cousin, the narcissistic style, is widely observed in the teen community, and its influence on teen life is everywhere to be seen.

My conclusions on this topic are not particularly profound, but they do have profound implications to anyone who seeks to understand the psychodynamics of adolescent behavior. It is my belief that the regression from developmental selfishness to narcissistic selfishness is a very real possibility during the course of the adolescent years. It does not occur with great regularity, but it does occur. This migration from natural to pathological selfishness is encouraged by our society's isolation of youth from real life, by its exclusion of youth from real responsibility, and by the endless barrage of narcissistic images hurled at youth by our consumerist, image-driven society. Because of the potential for this regression youth must be trained in the art of sociability, not merely because in its absence they have less civility, but because in the absence of this training the narcissistic attitudes inherent to adolescence elevate in power and assume a progressively greater role in the personality.

One of the insights which adolescent psychology has gathered from the study of narcissism and the narcissistic personality is that youth do not automatically, or even easily, learn the duties and responsibilities our society expects from them. Indeed, what we have discovered is that much within the adolescent personality actively resists the rights of others and the responsibilities of self. The ability of youth to honor their social obligations is determined not so much by their natural skills, their natural inclinations, or their natural predispositions, but, rather, by how effectively the adults in their lives have taught them, by word and by deed, to follow standards greater than those to which they are predisposed by age and inclination.

Anecdotes and Supplemental Information

[1]**Narcissistic selfishness.** What I call "narcissistic selfishness" resembles what H. Kohut and O. Kernberg called "pathological narcissism," and what Fred Alford called "regressive narcissism." To better understand the meaning behind narcissistic selfishness consider this:

In some of us, concerns with "narcissistic supplies," or supports to self-esteem, eclipse other issues to such an extent that we may be considered excessively self-preoccupied. Terms like "narcissistic personality" and pathological narcissism" apply to this disproportionate degree of self-concern, not to ordinary responsiveness to approval and sensitivity to criticism. (McWilliams, p. 170)

"Disproportionate degree of self-concern" is the issue in each of these three chapters on selfishness. As we shall see in the next chapter, the extreme, uncompromising, fear-driven selfishness we call "pathological selfishness," is a disproportionate exaggeration of the "narcissistic style." This is why we say that the narcissistic style can erode into pathological selfishness, and that developmental selfishness can erode into the narcissistic style.

[2]**Unhealthy narcisssim.** Otto Kernberg believed that unhealthy narcissism arises during early childhood, "as a result of chronically cold, unempathic parents who fail to provide the infant with the love and attention necessary for psychological health. Disruptions in the mother-child bond may bring about a refusion of self and object images, resulting in identity diffusion and an inflated or grandiose (narcissistic) self" (Berman, 1990, p. 24). Most theorists believe that in the narcissistic character the real self has never taken hold, therefore, the self-concept remains under the influence of childhood emotional states and the conflicts attendant to them. The more powerful these childhood emotional states, and the more primitive the conflicts within them, the stronger the narcissistic component to the personality.

[3]**Instrumental respect.** Individuals consumed with narcissistic selfishness may respect the feelings of others when it leads to their own gain or gratification. This is not to be confused with respect for people as people. Their respect is what behaviorists call "instrumental" respect since it is grounded in pragmatism more than in empathy, in receiving more than in giving, in utility more than in ideals. And, here again we draw to your attention that adolescents may be quite unprepared to draw distinctions between respect which is instrumental rather than genuine. Indeed, this is one of the

important aspects of friendship which must be negotiated during early-adolescence, and again, with the onset of romantic and erotic involvements, during late-adolescence.

[4]**Benefits of narrowness.** Another difference between narcissism and positive self-esteem is that the narcissistic character is actively engaged in narrowing and reducing the range of life experience. (Narcissism, unfailingly, is life-constraining not life-liberating; the criteria for life choices – self-gratification – is too narrow for self-liberation.) Since the narcissist's only real pleasure is in receiving praise and adulation, he (she) eliminates options that don't lead to praise and adulation. Narrowing the world is an attempt to eliminate everything beyond that which relates to one's private interests. The benefits of narrowness include the following.

• Narrowness lessens the pain of interacting with others who think of us as just another person.

• Narrowness is perceived as independence.

• Narrowness spotlights "me."

• Narrowness insulates against family expectations.

• Narrowness manipulates intimacy by declaring that it must be achieved in "my" territory and on "my" terms.

• Narrowness, at bottom, is emotional protectionism and a form of denying the value and importance of others – except as providers.

The romantic imagery of narcissistic youth (heroic isolation, splendorous solitude, one against the many, the slavish obedience of a loved one) often reduces to the simple formula of self towering over non-self.

Nine

The Rise of Narcissus in the Youth Culture

The selfishness of youth is a mystery to adults and to adolescents themselves; but it is such a mystery to modern psychology that virtually no one has bothered to deal with it in any systematic fashion during the past 60 years. This is a bit of a puzzle to me because in my career as an educator I have never met a single parent, a single teacher, or a single teen-ager who didn't believe that "selfishness," however it is variously defined, is a significant part of adolescent life.

Part of the problem, as we have seen in earlier chapters, is that "selfish" means different things to different people, and it expresses itself differently in different people. We have already discussed "developmental selfishness" and "pathological selfishness," and from this discussion we have learned something about healthy and unhealthy selfishness. We now need to take a further step to understand the selfishness so pervasive in our youth culture. To learn more about the "rise of Narcissus," we will look at the attitudes, the emotions and the behavior of "the narcissistic style."

Between the natural egoism of developmental self-ish-ness and the total self-obsession of narcissistic selfishness lives a third kind of selfishness which I call "the narcissistic style." In this chapter I will try to try to describe its essential features, and in so doing, I think we will see the differences between youth who are completely cloaked in self-priority and those who are not.

Before we begin, a brief step backwards might help us to better set our sights. Developmental selfishness refers to the natural self-centredness and to the necessary egoism which announces the adolescent personality. Narcissistic selfishness, in contrast, is a pathological selfishness resembling the Narcissistic Personality Disorder. The concept of narcissistic selfishness was introduced, not because I believe that it is a significant force in the adolescent community, but because I believe that its subdued version, the narcissistic style, is.

The narcissistic style is an *excessive swelling* of the selfishness natural to youth (also known as "developmental" selfishness), with a few additional twists. In addition to an exaggerated and persistent self-focus, the narcissistic style also carries with it a free-floating resentment which causes one to demean and degrade others. This combination of free floating resentment and the degradation of others (especially competitors) makes the extremes of the narcissistic style similar to the toxic narcissistic selfishness. However, the subdued expressions of the narcissistic style resemble the normal, developmental selfishness of youth. Hence, it is a matter of degree, but in this instance, degree is everything.

The narcissistic style begins with the normal selfishness of youth, but it is encouraged and accelerated by the narcissistic qualities of the dominant culture and the self-ish qualities of teen culture. The narcissistic style moves the young person away from normal psychological functioning toward dysfunction, away from normal selfishness toward profound selfishness.

My concern in this chapter is with the mental and emotional habits associated with the narcissistic style. My comments do not include firm and final statements about origins – those I gladly leave to the theoreticians. (As I tried to indicate earlier, a clear explanation of the origins of narcissism requires one to accept as fact numerous unverified assumptions.)[1]

I have no doubt about the pervasiveness of the narcissistic style in the adolescent population, and neither, if my assessment is correct, do most teachers, coaches, social workers, clergy, and parents. The narcissistic style is a particularly meddlesome condition because it acquires its strength during adolescence, a time of life for moving away from the egocentric narrowness of childhood toward the more allocentric openness and community mindedness of mature adulthood, and participatory democracy. The narcissistic style thwarts this natural transformation by imbuing the adolescent with a relentless egotism which subtracts from mutuality and adds to self-priority. The narcissistic style dampens the sense of community awareness required of civil community.

With these preliminary comments serving as our guide, let us now take a more detailed look at the habits and reflexes of "the narcissistic style."

The Narcissistic Style in the Community of Teens

The defining feature of the narcissistic style is an egotism which exceeds normal developmental boundaries, but does not equal the outrageous excesses of narcissistic selfishness. The narcissistic style inhabits an in-between world with developmental selfishness on one border and narcissistic selfishness on the other, showing itself sometimes as exaggerated developmental selfishness, and at other times as subdued narcissistic selfishness.

Rueben Fine once claimed "All people are narcissistic; the difference is only one of degree." To this Fred Alford added: "Although pathological narcissism sounds so sick . . . healthy narcissism shares many of the same characteristics . . . This is explained by a presumption . . . shared by almost all theorists of narcissism that there is a continuum between pathological and normal narcissism . . . (Alford, 1988, p. 70). If one accepts the idea that narcissism exists on a continuum from healthy to pathological, the narcissistic style is found near the mid-point.

In the remainder of this chapter there will be a description of the emotional and mental habits of the narcissistic style. The focus is on five basic traits which, in their totality, make up the profile of the narcissistic style. They include:

- expectations of entitlements

- deadness to the feelings and rights of others

- reduced capacity to *give* love

- reduced moral circumference, and,

- reduced ability to think objectively.

The Expectation of Entitlements

> . . . they operate on the fantastic assumption that their mere desire is justification for possessing whatever they seek. (Theodore Millon)

One of the more irritating presumptions of individuals who live by the code of the narcissistic style is their belief that it is the responsibility of others to look after "me" and "my" needs. Individuals who exhibit this attitude expect far more from others than is reasonable, and they demand far more from their school, their government, and their family than can reasonably be delivered. They view their parents, their schools, and their governments as providers, and when they fail to provide they are viewed with anger and contempt. Adolescents obsessed with such expectations do not even faintly recognize how objectionable their attitude is to their parents, their teachers, indeed, to all of their "providers."

An attitude of entitlement leads youth to believe that they should be admitted to a theatre after it is sold out, should be given permission to take an examination late when such permission is granted to no other students. Boys charged with entitlement may believe that they are entitled to the affection, loyalty, or sexual favors of a girl they know, or date, or with whom they simply share a classroom. When these expectations are not satisfied, the boy may pout, hold a grudge, or slander the girl who failed to deliver. Entitlement-driven individuals are not easily rebuffed because they presume their expectations and demands are perfectly natural and completely justified.

It is widely held that an attitude of entitlement is encouraged by the family and the school (the two most important institutions in the lives of the young), both of whom grant a wide range of benefits but set few requirements for how to function in return. That is to say, benefits are in place, but obligations are not. There is little doubt that in our present society adolescents live under a regime of social values that allows them to make demands on family, school, and society-at-large far more than vice versa. From this tradition of being able to make demands without having to accept duties and responsibilities the entitlement mentality grows.

Hans Sebald contributed to the dialogue which examines the entitlement mentality, and some of his ideas speak to what we are discussing here.

> . . . young Americans remain relatively unimpressed by the economic crisis and somehow seem to assume that some satisfactory economic security will materialize for them. This is not so much personal optimism as it is a new *philosophy of entitlement* anchored in the burgeoning American welfare state... a curious conversion of wants and desires into presumed "rights" . . . The desire "I'd like a secure income" becomes "I am entitled to a secure income." While the tendency to feel righteous about one's desires is natural and has been with us for a long time, *the equation of desire with right has grown significantly in the current generation.* (1984, p. 245)

He has more to say on the youthful expectation of entitlement.

> The attitude can be summed up as the "philosophy of entitlement," referring to the development of a pervasive feeling of being entitled to all sorts of material and psychological benefits and that the provision of these benefits is the responsibility of society. (Sebald, p. 19)

Entitlement turns social responsibility upside down with the claim that the group is completely responsible for looking after "me." This premise, while foreign to anyone with a social conscience, is completely reasonable to (a) young children, (b) anxious and immature adolescents, (c) adult narcissists. It requires minimal teaching to take hold; to teach the entitlement mentality to a child is the easiest task any teacher could have.

Entitlement obsession also contradicts the basic tenets of altruism. "Almost all societies, from the most primitive to the most civilized, have emphasized duties much more than rights or liberties, and almost all of their members have accepted these duties without protest" (Muller, 1960, p. 26). The present discussion is not the proper forum for a thorough analysis of Muller's ideas, but it is a good place to reflect on possible connections, especially if we see merit in his point that in every society (including the society of youth) dignified survival depends, at least in part, on a sense of duty and responsibility to the group.

The narcissistic style shares commonalities with the behavior of children; the dynamics are different, but behavior is surprisingly similar. To emphasize this I share with you a little poem, written by Elisa Morgan, which I use in my university course in child psychology to bring home the egocentricity of the toddler. Here it serves a purpose other than the author intended, but, if you have any narcissistic companions, you will see them in her poem about toddlers.

The Toddler's Creed

If I want it, it's mine.

If I give it to you and change

my mind later, it's mine.

If I can take it away from you,

it's mine.

If I had it a little while ago,

it's mine.

If it's mine

it will never belong to anyone else.

If we are building something together,

all of the pieces are mine.

If it looks just like mine,

it is mine.

Entitlement-driven individuals assume that their beliefs are *inherently truthful* merely because they believe them. The beliefs of others are given no such *carte blanche;* they are viewed with skepticism, and must be defended by solid evidence. Entitlement thinkers employ a completely unfair system of intellectual accountability where others must defend their ideas as in a court of law, and where their own ideas are truthful *a priori.* All in all, entitlement thinkers operate on the premise that "I" am right, but "you" must prove your ideas beyond a reasonable doubt. This attitude makes reasoned debate impossible.

What we come to is this: an attitude of entitlement is the first symptom of the narcissistic style. It presumes that "I" deserve out-of-the ordinary favors, and that it is "your" responsibility to provide them. These individuals ascribe Divine Right to themselves; they don't require proper grounds for their claims as they themselves are proper grounds. They have extra rights because they are extra special; the exceptionalism they profess is warranted by their own exceptionality. Or so it seems to them.[3]

One can see what a comfortable fit is fashioned between the attitude of entitlement and narcissism. Each justifies and reinforces the other.

Deadness to the Feelings of Others

The worst sin towards our fellow creatures is not to hate them, but to be indifferent to them: that's the essence of inhumanity. (George Bernard Shaw)

Certain psychologists who have a prejudice against facing up to the self-ish side of human nature contend that people act selfishly only when they are required to do so, or when the rewards for selfishness greatly exceed its punishment, or when only slight chance exists for being caught. While I respect the scholars who hold these views, I find no evidence in my experience to support them. Indeed, as far as adolescents are concerned, I find their line of thinking not only naive, but preposterous.[2] Adolescent selfishness is as natural as childhood selfishness; it doesn't need to be learned because it is inherent to the personality, but learning can lessen or strengthen its force.

Emotional deadness is not rare among teens. Teachers see it daily in youngsters who, when confronted with a wrongdoing, claim they didn't do it. Or, yes, they did it, but they couldn't help it; or, yes they did it, but they didn't know they were doing it; or yes, they did it, but so what. Sometimes they don't know what they have done, and at other times they simply disown their actions; an unwelcome mixture of alienation and defiance.

When confronted by a teacher for rules violations, they claim their behavior wasn't bad because they didn't *intend* anything bad. They act "as-if" motives are more important than actions. Such behavior-deadening was conveyed by a sixteen-year-old boy I once interviewed in a youth detention centre, incarcerated after he shot another teen with a hand gun concealed in his jacket. To him it was unfair that he had to serve time because he didn't intend to shoot the victim. "He just sort of got in the way." He intended to shoot a member of a rival gang, but "this other dude just started shoving and gettin' involved where he didn't have any right. I shot him but it was no big deal. I didn't even mean to shoot him. If I shot `D,' like I wanted to, then they would have a case. Just 'cuz some guy gets in the way. It's really more like an accident. I don't think I should do time for that."

These youngsters hide from their own unacceptable behavior with the claim that it is their intentions (not their behavior) that should be judged. Their logic is simple, though bent: "You can't punish me for what I didn't intend to do." Or, "You can't punish me for what I couldn't prevent." (We gain a certain insight into the narcissistic style when we recognize that these youngsters *never* accept this claim when it is made to them by others).

When their relationships turn sour, when exploited friends complain or simply walk out, when parents tell them they are sick of being their servants, they are usually taken by complete surprise. Unbalanced relationships are so compatible with their nature that it does not occur to them that their partners feel exploited. From these youngsters we repeatedly hear: "I can't believe you're telling me this"; "How come you are suddenly saying this?"; "Why didn't you tell me you feel this way?"

Youngsters enveloped in a narcissistic style have slanted perceptions of adults because they evaluate them by whether they are flattered by them. Most generally, they "respect" adults who praise them, but they have "no respect whatsoever" for those who don't. In their judgments of adults, they are incapable of rendering an independent verdict. Basically, they like adults who praise them, and dislike those who don't. They dignify their like or dislike with the word "respect," but the truth is that respect has almost nothing to do with it.[4] They ridicule adults who don't show them attention, because such an adult is, to them, ridiculous. Among their peers these adult-rejecting teens may attain a great deal of acclaim because of their ability to make administrators look like buffoons, teachers idiots, police Nazis, psychologists neurotics.

In sum, deadness to the feelings of others further entrenches the narcissistic style by distancing youth from the human-ness of peers (and adults) with whom they share their social world.[5]

The Reduced Capacity to Give Love

> The most grievous cost of a narcissistic orientation is a stunted capacity to love. (Nancy McWilliams)

Teens imbued with a narcissistic style need love, but, for reasons we do not completely understand, their expectations are greatly overloaded on the receiving end. Their pressing urge is to *receive* love, and all of their energy is directed to this end. Their main pleasure is in receiving, so they are bored when no new sources feed them. Here we see one of their many contradictions: their *need* for others is deep, but their love for them is shallow. This aspect of their nature doesn't hurt them much in adolescence because, for the most part, teens don't distinguish between the two. Girls, in particular, may ind a boy's need for them proof that the boy loves them.

Narcissistic youth import, but do not export, love. Indeed, love with a narcissist, is, by any dignified use of the word, impossible. Reciprocity and mutuality, the heart and soul of mature intimacy, cannot be when one of the partners is chronically narcissistic.

How then, taking their selfish qualities into account, do they attract others into their sphere? How do they get peers to like them? To fall in love with them? These questions are investigated in greater detail in a later chapter, so for the moment, a cursory overview will suffice. Basically, it works like this. Individuals with a narcissistic style idealize, glorify, and glamorize those who provide them with emotional supplies; they court affection by convincing their suppliers that it is *they* who are loved when, in reality, it is what they supply that is loved. Their friends believe that it is they who are loved.

The underlying cause of their failure to give love is unclear, but most theorists who investigate the emotional infrastructure of narcissism believe that it derives either from the numbing pain of childhood rejection, or smoldering resentment from being insufficiently loved. But what these theorists fail to recognize is that during adolescence, selfishness can be triggered merely by the desire to consume. "Why give when you can receive?" is the motto of every egocentric; it is simply carried to greater extremes in the narcissistic style.

Narcissistic individuals do not seek human relationships where give and take exist in fair proportion; rather, they seek relationships in which their partners shower endless admiration upon them without demanding much in return. They prefer flattering mirrors (see Chapter Ten) to genuine friends.

What we have thus far uncovered about the narcissistic style is that it is an approach to life obsessed with entitlements, insensitive to the feelings of others, and driven by the need to receive love without giving much in return. There is more.

Reduced Moral Circumference

To make your children capable of honesty is the beginning of education. (John Ruskin)

Moral diminishment is a subject which has not been studied with sufficient care in traditional psychology. It is with some trepidation that I put forth any ideas on the topic; yet it is so relevant to the narcissistic style that I feel compelled to do so.

Morality, by definition, requires the alignment of one's actions and beliefs *with a principle or a standard greater than oneself.* Such alignment is inherently difficult for individuals for whom morality is determined by their own needs. This does not mean that they do not believe in good or bad; it means that what they think of as "good" and what they think of as "bad" is determined by whether it favors or disfavors them. Narcissistic morality is a brew of pragmatism and egotism rather than a genuine moral system. For these reasons the morality that we usually see in the narcissistic style is *moralization –* morality grounded in rationalization. It parallels the primitive morality of preschoolers who believe that whatever favors them is right, and whatever disfavors them is wrong.

Rights, responsibilities, and the narcissistic style. The social contracts which bind children to their parent society might seem straightforward, but they are not. Our society is presently locked in debate about the relative weight of rights and obligations. Billions of education and welfare dollars are appropriated, in great measure, by our understanding of how much we owe youth, and how much they owe us. The debate is heated because some of us believe that the entitlements of youth outweigh their responsibilities, while others believe their responsibilities outweigh their entitlements.

We, as a society, do not agree on the actions youth are morally obligated to perform. What duty do they owe their parents? What labor should youth be required to perform? Are youth obligated to show respect or deference to adults? To what extent are youth accountable? Accountable to whom or to what? To what degree can we expect young people to know right from wrong, to be punished for wrongdoing, or rewarded for doing right? Do the responsibilities of youth require them to meet their financial obligations? Can we rightfully expect them to be morally responsible for the consequences of their sexual behavior, financially responsible in their economic transactions, parentally responsible for the children they produce, legally responsible for the people they injure on the highways?

On the other side of the coin: What are the just and fair claims of youth? What are they entitled to by law, by nature, by merit of being young? What claims can they make "in their own right"? Much of the debate reduces to one key question: Should rights or duties hold greater sway during adolescence?

Rights are difficult to discuss because in many people's thinking they are prefaced by "inalienable," which translates into "guaranteed," and by "my," which translates into "not necessarily yours." Perhaps no concept, philosophical or legal, is as subject to as much narcissistic bending as rights. To teach teens about their rights is an easy task, but to teach them their duties, the rights of others, is more difficult. No one has expressed the narcissistic view of duties more concisely than Oscar Wilde, himself a self-admitted narcissist. "Duty is what one expects from others – it is not what one does oneself."

Painfully, youth obsessed with their own rights tend to be indifferent to the rights of others. Some critics believe that youth in the 21st century are less able to take care of themselves and less willing to respect the rights of others than in earlier decades. They cannot take care of themselves, yet at the same time, they do not respect those who provide for them; they are desensitized to others but hypochondriacally self-sensitive; they are rude but demand to be treated courteously. All of which amounts to a form of citizen infantilism.

From these remarks it will be seen that the narcissistic style, in addition to its attitude of entitlement, its deadness to the feelings of others, its reduced capacity to give love, is deepened by an under-developed morality.

Reduced Intellectual Objectivity

The narcissistic person then, ends up with an enormous distortion. He and his are overevaluated. Everything outside is underevaluated. The damage to reason and objectivity is obvious. (Erich Fromm)

The narcissistic attitude has a crushing effect on clear thinking because in it intelligence works full time defending its owner.

A person, to the extent to which he is narcissistic, has a double standard of perception. Only he himself and what pertains to him has significance, while the rest of the world is more or less weightless or colorless, and because of this double standard *the narcissistic person shows severe defects in judgment and lacks the capacity for objectivity.* (Fromm, 1973, p. 148)

The narcissistic style shows its true colors when the object of thought pertains to worth, superiority, shame, envy, glory, competence, beauty, acceptance, achievement, or desirability. In other words, whenever thought impinges on self-esteem. The narcissistic style poses no real problem when the thinker is investigating an emotion-free zone such as wheat production in China, the internet, the Dow Jones average, assuming that none of these topics is close to one's emotional centre. The narcissistic style is designed to protect and elevate; when there is no need, the intellect operates freely and objectively. This is why intellectual performance is so uneven among individuals imbued with the narcissistic style; on one topic the intellect freely uses all of its resources, on another it is bogged in protection and defense. Twist and turn as we may, we cannot escape the fact that the narcissistic style impedes objective thinking; it is grounded in self-protection, not reality.

What Does All of This Mean?

I conceive that when a man deliberates whether he shall do a thing or not do it, he does nothing else but consider whether it is better for himself to do it or not to do it. (Thomas Hobbes)

Thomas Hobbes is not the philosopher of choice much anymore, except among political theorists and military strategists. In the community of narcissists, however, he would probably be voted "Most likely to succeed." His calculated utilitarianism, and suspicious mistrust, is tailor-made for the narcissistic style. But, one might ask "Does he speak to all youth?"

As to the progression from childhood egocentrism to narcissistic selfishness, the evidence from developmental psychology, and the social psychology of youth, suggests that this progression comes so easily that one can think of it as natural.[6] This comes as no surprise to anyone familiar with normal growth trends. We know that children do not learn all things with equal ease. If you doubt this, try teaching a group of children to be left-handed, or to choose celery over sweets; then, try to teach a group of children to be right-handed and to choose sweets over celery. These are not equal tasks. The predispositions which children bring to their experience shape their preferences, their inclinations, and what they *easily* learn. To teach selfish attitudes and self-serving habits to children (and adolescents) is one of the easiest assignments one could possibly have because their personality is laced with a compatible egocentrism.

There is really not much doubt about the emotional predispositions of youth. Their egocentrism, their developmental selfishness, and their natural impulses for survival and self-preservation, taken in combined strength, incline them to self-priority. The narcissistic style is easily learned when glorified in popular culture, or rewarded in peer culture, and even more so when youth are untrained to reject the human diminishment which comes with it.

I would like to make clear that all of the problems of youth are not caused by the narcissistic style, but I also want to make clear that all problems of youth are deepened by it.[7]

All teens live in a community but they have remarkably little sense of community. In North American teen culture, there are few worthwhile projects to invest one's decency, and few worthy people with whom to share higher yearnings. One outcome of this imbalance is an obsession with self without an underlying appreciation for the self, and a disrespect for others without an underlying knowledge of them.

We keep returning to a fundamental principle: youth who do not find a worthy someone in whom to invest their hopes, who do not build, who do not volunteer their energy and their spirit, and who do not contribute to the well-being of others are prime candidates for an increase in selfishness and a lifestyle of self-priority; as far as the themes of this chapter are concerned, they are candidates for the regressive slide from developmental selfishness into the narcissistic style.

Anecdotes and Supplemental Information

[1]**Freud and Adler on human nature**. What we are here discussing (the origins of selfishness in human nature) was a source of great conflict between Sigmund Freud and Alfred Adler in their thirty-year debate on the particulars of human nature. When Freud originated the concept of narcissism he had in mind "a protective channeling of energy into the self, a healthy self-interest or self-love." Adler postulated (and in this regard his thought is much closer to Karen Horney's than to Sigmund Freud's) that narcissism is an obsessive inward fixation which maximizes self-concern and diminishes social interest. To Adler, the narcissistic attitude is not innate or instinctual, it is a learned response. Adler's version of narcissism explores the selfish expressions of narcissism (such as entitlement demands) since he recognized from the beginning that narcissism leads one away from social interest in order to more efficiently pursue one's own needs, cravings, and desires.

[2]**Egoism.** Arthur Schopenhauer (who grappled with the inherently selfish qualities within our being as tenaciously as any of the pre-Freudian thinkers) once claimed: "Egoism is so deeply rooted a quality of all individuals in general, that in order to rouse the activity of an individual being, egotistical ends are the only ones upon which we count with certainty." Schopenhauer's statement has been debated in many quarters, but whether one accepts or rejects his view of human nature, no one doubts that many of us are motivated exactly as he described.

[3]**Entitlement thinkers abhor impartiality.** Why? Because impartiality means fairness, and fairness means I do not have an advantage. Teens embroiled in the narcissistic style resent fairness. (Gender equity, for example). If you want to discourage a narcissistic friend show him impartiality, objectivity, evenhandedness; soon he will be gone. Narcissists cannot survive in an atmosphere of fairness because it opposes the defining need of their personality – the need to be favored, the need to be chosen, the need to be "greater than."

[4]**Respect.** Narcissists are obsessed with "respect," but their understanding of it has little to do with its real meaning. To show respect is to acknowledge the basic integrity or worthiness of a person; to show consideration; to treat with deference. To youngsters gripped by the narcissistic attitude, *respect* means to flatter, to inflate. Integrity has little to do with what narcissists call "respect." When narcissists complain that so-and-so "shows no respect," we discover that the person does not overly praise or artificially inflate. The adolescent obsession with "respect" amounts to little more than contrived ingratiation; it rarely has to do with integrity.

[5]**The soloist and the choir.** Harold D. Grovetant, in an informative essay on adolescent identity, subtitled his essay "Bringing the soloist to the choir." In this article he puts forth ideas which share commonalities with ideas put forth here, especially, the tenet that every young self is engaged in a struggle to balance the legitimate needs and demands of the group with the legitimate needs and demands of "me." The key words, however, are not "group" and "me," rather "balance" and "integration." Grovetant writes: "Metaphorically, the interplay required for musicians to produce a coherent, balanced performance is not unlike the interplay required for the orchestration of one's sense of personal identity; both involve blending and integration" (1993, p. 121). Individuals steeped in narcissism enjoy their role as soloists but they fail to grasp that without the choir they have no place to sing. For them "balance" and "integration" mean something quite different than to the choir members, who view the soloist as one voice in a chorus of many.

[6]**Egocentrism and narcissism**. Taking into account our earlier discussion of egocentrism one might be inclined to think that the narcissistic attitude and egocentrism amount to the same thing. This is not so.

The egocentrism natural to children predisposes them to anticipate that they will be favored. To young children it is natural that mother provides them with special gifts, even when it requires great sacrifice on her part. Egocentrism predisposes children to anticipate that they will be blessed with good fortune, that they will receive the benefit of doubt, and that they will routinely have exceptions made on their behalf. These anticipations permeate their demeanor so completely that when formal thought begins to impress upon them the need for impartiality, it implodes their belief that they will always receive the lion's share in every dispute. The predisposition to think that events *will* fall in one's favor is the precursor to thinking that things *should* fall in one's favor. The difference between egocentrism and narcissism is the difference between "is" and "should."

The anticipation of good news is tempered by reason, common sense, and evidence. So, to give a simple example, the child's anticipation that he will receive most of the candy is easily brought into line with father's ruling that the candy will be divided evenly. The egocentricity which governs the lives of children is usually reduced by all forms of communication in which the desires of one person come into conflict with those of another.

To summarize: the egocentrism of children is not the same as the narcissistic style of adolescence even though they share the common features of self-embeddedness and self-priority. Narcissism is richer in its emotionality, more hostile in its resentments, and more emotive in its self-defense than egocentrism. All narcissists are egocentric but not all egocentrics are narcissists.

[7]Narcissism and social interest. In psychological circles the undisputed champion of the belief that humans are predisposed to share and cooperate is Alfred Adler. David Hume once claimed, "There is some benevolence, however small, infused into our bosom, some spark of friendship for human kind, some particle of the dove kneaded into our frame, along with the elements of the serpent and the wolf." Alfred Adler went much further; he believed that "the spark of friendship for human kind," and the "dove kneaded into our frame," were, in fact, the dominant features of human nature, and to him the "serpent and the wolf" are but necessary inventions to protect our vulnerable selves from a callous, sometimes brutal, environment. Adler believed that all humans possess inborn predispositions for sharing and cooperation which translate into an active propensity toward fellowship and supportive companionship. He was the first of the psychodynamic theorists to claim that we receive greater satisfaction being helpful than being helped, and that all of us desire to assist our fellow citizens and to build human community.

Adler believed that it is easy to cultivate a compassionate nature in youth because they are naturally inclined to give their cooperation and to express their empathy. He rejected Freud's theory of narcissism, since it could not explain cooperation, sharing, volunteerism, or the broad spectrum of "giving without taking" we observe in all human communities. Adler eventually came to believe that excessive striving for selfish goals is a neurotic distortion of our inborn impulse to cooperate. All in all, Adler's concept of social interest is the diametric opposite of narcissistic selfishness. Whether selfishness comes into being, as Adler suggested, from the blunting of social interest, is a matter still debated by the well informed, and not to be settled here.

"Social interest," as used by Adler, is a translation from the German word "Gemeinschaftsgefuhl," which means "social feeling" or "community feeling." Adler used it to mean a pervasive feeling of attachment to all humanity and membership in the social community of all people. In Adler's understanding of human nature, social interest manifests itself as a natural, inborn impulse toward cooperation. Adler believed that social interest is an inherent part of human nature which exists as potential. It does not spring forth fully blossomed; it is encouraged through parental love, guidance, and sharing during the first five years of life. From these early interactions comes the desire to contribute to society.

Because of our hypotheses concerning the egocentric and the narcissistic predispositions of adolescents, it is abundantly clear that Adler's theory of social interest is not our starting point. However, without going into it at this moment, it should also be clear that Adler's ideas are vital to our deliberations on this topic. Why? From our investigations of adolescence, a fundamental principle emerges: youth lacking social interest are left with nothing to guide them except their narcissism. "Only those persons who are really trained in the direction of social interest . . . will actually have social feeling." "Social feeling," as Adler rightly observed, is not an inevitable fact of life; like speech, or even walking, the mechanics are provided by nature, but the environment must provide some training if they are to develop.

Ten

Social Survival

Of all the things which wisdom provides to make life entirely happy, much the greatest is the possession of friendship. (Epicurus)

Friendship, adolescent style, is not all fun and games. It has its human side, and its business side, and often it is difficult for the adolescent, much less the outside observer, to tell which is which. This chapter looks at some of the tough challenges of adolescent social life, the motives behind them, and the intelligence which tries to make sense out of them.

The desire for friendship springs from emotions and needs, but the ground rules which regulate it are drafted by the intelligence. Since "loyalty," "fairness," "friendship," and "faithful" all have a definitional (hence cerebral) component, we cannot fully appreciate adolescent friendship without taking into account the intelligence which does the defining and the morality which does the justifying.

From our earlier look at the thought process, we have seen that adolescent thinking is swayed by peer acceptance and rejection, by fear, fables, and narcissism. These essentially irrational forces exert considerable influence on adolescent friendship. They do not *determine* the nature of friendship, but they leave a recognizable stamp on it. Countering these irrational forces stands an impressive stable of intellectual strengths including the capacity for introspection and self-analysis, consequence testing, and a growing talent for propositional thought. During adolescence, all friendships, whether they are superficial or intimate, exploitive or fair, utilitarian or ideal, acquire their defining qualities from these rational and irrational forces.

The heart and soul of teen social survival is learning to balance the dignity of the self with the benefits of the peer group. Now, without pledging ourselves in any way to adopt this hypothesis, let us dally with it for a while to see to what consequences it might lead if it were true.

The Nature of Friendship During Adolescence

Without friends, no one would choose to live. (Aristotle)

Real friendship is no easy thing at any age, and those who see it as natural to adolescence miss the boat. Most adolescents have friends, to be sure, but there is nothing guaranteed nor automatic about friendship during the teen years. Many kids have no friends, and some have more than they have time for, but whether teens have many or few friends, during this time of life friendship has more of a survivalist flavor than most adults recognize.[1]

For starters, most adolescent peer groups are grounded in forces which have little to do with genuine friendship, including the ABCs of peer survival – accommodating, blending, and cooperating. Genuine friendship takes time, effort, and considerable sacrifice. Simply hanging out and being together doesn't do it. The bonding which grows from hanging out and being together is, most assuredly, a form of friendship, but a primitive one. Most early-adolescents do not possess a very clear understanding of affiliation bonding, and they frequently confuse it with deeper forms of friendship, or even with love. Older teens have a deeper understanding of friendship, they know how precious (and elusive) real friendship is; perhaps this is why they idealize it so richly, and why it always works its way to the top of their wish list.

All youngsters need friendship, companionship, and love. These needs drive the adolescent's social world, but they are complicated by an elementary point: while teens need meaningful relationships, they have difficulty forming them because of their limited experience, their lack of necessary social skills, and their limited ability to comprehend the personhood of others. These developmental shortcomings get in the way of friendship, especially deep friendship. Perhaps this is why Louise Kaplan claimed that "new loves and friendships," for most adolescents, "*usually prove to be unstable, transient, and heartbreakingly disappointing* "(1984, p. 151).

When we look closely at the adolescent's social world, we see that it is more a collection of cliques and informal alliances than a real community. Indeed, it is precisely the narrowness of teen concerns and their minimal breadth of human connections, which makes clique rejection and alliance retaliation such a devastating experience.[2]

Friendship is no easy thing even at the best of times, but it is especially difficult when the partners have difficulty placing themselves in another's shoes, and when they are not yet ready to cope with the very real demands of emotional reciprocity. Take *respect*, for example. Adolescents make a great deal of respect, and rightly so, but their understanding of it is so burdened by narcissistic niggling that, in teen culture, the word has devolved into a loose synonym for deference or subservience. Respect, framed in narcissistic narrowness, has little to do with equality, fairness, or personal dignity. What passes for "respect" in most teen cliques amounts to little more than ritualized flattery.

Respect, of course, means something completely different among individuals of more mature identity and more autonomous self-esteem. Healthy respect includes an honest sensitivity to the unique features of the respected person, and an acknowledgment of that person's basic integrity. It has many faces. Respect for a partner's beliefs implies sensitive listening and sympathetic responses; respect for a partner's talents means encouraging ambitions and supporting endeavors and, as well, appreciating achievements; respect for the partner's rights means recognizing freedom and liberty, and encouraging them; respect for the partner's privacy means not sulking when the partner requires solitude or isolation.

Respect, simple as it sounds, is an *achievement* which requires mental and emotional maturity, an independent intelligence, and a set of beliefs about what is worthy and what isn't. On these counts younger adolescents usually come up short, and that is why they not only have trouble giving and receiving respect in their daily relationships, they have trouble understanding the concept in the first place.

Along the adolescent friendship path we see many breakups, and, all things considered, this is not such a bad thing. Adolescence, after all, is an age for experimentation, for exploration, and for sampling relationships unknown during the protected sanctuary of childhood. Rarely are these experiments completely successful. Some of them are downright disastrous. For youth who learn from such encounters, adolescence can be a productive internship for the more emotionally demanding responsibilities of early adulthood.

In this chapter we will look at some of the reasons why adolescents, even though they crave friendship, belonging, and love, have trouble satisfying these basic human needs consistently and meaningfully.[3]

Social Survival in the Teen Community

The worst solitude is to be destitute of sincere friendship. (Francis Bacon)

Speaking in broad terms, we can say that adolescent friendships are of three types. The first can be thought of as "friendships of pleasure," in which the partners enjoy each other's company, derive pleasure from it, and each partner adds to the happiness of the other. The second can be thought of as "friendship of utility," in which the association between two individuals benefits each other in a variety of practical ways, and as a result, certain goals and ambitions are better satisfied because of the friendship. Utility friendships are consequence driven, which is to say that outcomes go a long way in determining the success of the friendship. These friendships thrive in group settings where individuals share duties and responsibilities – the workplace, school, dormitories, sports teams, etc. The third type of friendship is that of "reciprocity and mutuality;" friendships where partners show genuine concern for each others needs, for each other's long term welfare, and where the partners enjoy mutual admiration. This kind of friendship weathers misfortune rather well because its connections are sincere and not excessively weighted by the narcissism which typifies "pleasure" and "utility" friendship. Reciprocity and mutuality friendship can be thought of as the highest form of adolescent friendship, in that it requires honesty and intimacy usually lacking in pleasure and utility friendships. It serves as the advance guard of mature intimacy and love.

The friendships of early- and middle-adolescents are primarily of the first two types: pleasure and utility. From a developmental perspective this is perfectly since deeper expressions of friendship are, generally speaking, beyond the maturational level of early-to-mid teens.[4] Part of what I am trying to convey was first introduced to modern adolescent psychology by Edgar Friedenberg in his classic work, *The Vanishing Adolescent*. Friedenberg was fully aware that adolescents are not angelic, that they often behave like self-serving junior executives, and that the cement which holds them together is not always mortared by ideal friendship. He helped us to recognize that adolescent friendship tends to be situational, need-driven, and necessity grounded. His insights aren't flattering to youth, but they aren't wrong either.

> Groups of juveniles are not friendly; and strong-felt friendships do not commonly form among them, though there is often constant association between members of juvenile cliques. They are not there to be friendly; they are there to work out a crude social system and to learn the ropes from one another. To some extent they behave like the gang in an office, jockeying for position within a superficially amiable social group. (1959, p. 44)

In sum, adolescent conformity to the peer group is motivated as much by necessity as enjoyment. Friedenberg recognized three important principles of adolescent life overlooked by the current crop of experts. First, there are important differences between friendly and friendship, a distinction rarely made in current literature. Second, among the young sociability may derive as much from the setting as from the human qualities of the person with whom a relationship is shared. Third, while togetherness brings laughter and deep emotion, these experiences are not the same as real friendship. As Friedenberg recognized almost half a century ago, the adolescent peer group is a group of peers, but not necessarily a group of friends. Indeed, coming to recognize the difference between a peer and a friend is one of the basic tasks of adolescence, and those who do not succeed in it encounter a fresh set of difficulties with early-adulthood and the intimacy usually required of it.

•   •   •

A relevant research project speaks to the main ideas I am trying to assemble here in my look at social survival among teens. Sue Lees (1986) investigated teen friendships first-hand, interviewing adolescent girls over a five year period, and in doing so distilled a more personal assessment of adolescent friendship than is usually reported in the psychological literature. (Freidenberg, it should be pointed out, did not base his conclusions about adolescent life on data gathered from teens as much as from his personal insights into the adolescent personality and how it operates within its social world). Lees was primarily concerned with *how power relations shape the adolescent experience*, especially for girls; her strategy was "to take the girls' own descriptions and raise questions about the way they describe their lives, their experiences, their relationships . . ." (p. 157).

One of Lees' more intriguing findings was how teen friendships are burdened with grinding antagonisms and uneasy alliances. Although the girls in her study very much desired genuine intimacy, mutual admiration, and true love, they faced a day-to-day social world laced with stinging demands on acceptance, popularity, and reputation. Lees reported that all of the girls she interviewed agreed that friendship means loyalty and sticking up for your friend. However, it is never that straightforward: "The other side of the coin is bitching and spreading gossip and rumors. Bitching is constantly referred to as something that girls are particularly adept at and as the source of aggravation and even fights among girls" (p. 65). One girl says: "Sue, one moment she can be really nice but the next moment she can be really bitchy. Sue will use what you say against you." Another girl reports: "There are boys that bitch as well – but on the whole I think girls have more character for bitching." Another says: "Girls get pretty ratty and annoyed with each other and say things about each other. Whereas boys . . . don't bitch about each other behind each other's backs so much."

The adolescent community, as described by teens themselves, is one in which the all too human failings of betrayal, gossip, and slander are facts of daily life:

> That's why you have to be careful who you hang around with, who you speak to, because even the slightest thing you tell them, they can change what you said and get you into a lot of trouble. You might say something to them, 'Don't tell anyone what I just told you.' The next morning the whole school knows it. (Lees, p. 68)

The condemnation of peers (the same ones who also serve as friends) which flows so freely in teen groups is driven by an elementary code of juvenile competition: that which cannot be won over is demonized. "One reason why so few girls talk even to their closest friends about sexual desire or actual sexual behavior is through fear that their friend might betray them and gossip – spread the rumor that they were a slag [promiscuous]" (Lees, p. 68). Slander is everyday fare: "A more vicious type of devaluing aspects of other girls is to cast doubt on their sexual reputation, which is why much of the bitching characterized by girls involves slander" (p. 66). According to one subject in the study, girls who desire a boy-friend but have difficulty attracting boys are the most bitchy. Lees suggests that "bitchiness seems to be a way of devaluing aspects of other girls that you wish to signal as `not you'. It is a way of marking differences between other girls and yourself." One girl, describing herself says: "I am bitchy. I say `oh she's so fat'. You say it in front of friends for instance to see if they say `You can't talk, you're just as fat' or to see if they agree with you." What is at stake here should not be taken lightly. In the teen world reputation is currency, and anything which inflates or deflates it is big business. "An attack on a girl's reputation is an attack on her personal morality and integrity which only she can defend" (Lees, p. 72).

I do not want to convey an exaggerated impression of the trials and tribulations of teen life; neither, however, do I desire that this book join the stream of sterile treatises which claim to describe the adolescent experience but instead give the reader nothing more than a Pollyanna vision of teen society which sees all youth problems as caused by unloving parents, by incompetent teachers, or by oppressive rules. Youth have their own frailties, their own limitations, and their own deficiencies which account for most of their storm and stress. None of us benefit from denying this fact of their nature.

The social toughness and the mean-spiritedness observed by virtually all investigators who actually participate in the lives of youth (rather than those researchers who merely report the results of paper-pencil tests) harken to mind Mark Twain's chide: "It takes your enemy and friend, working together, to hurt you to the heart; the one to slander you, and the other to get the news to you." I think that one of the reasons so many adolescents like Twain is because he accepted outright the raw realities of human bondings, and he knew that in every friendship there is a touch of the angel, and a bit of the devil.

Rejection, the Fear of Rejection, and the Consequences of Rejection

The most pervasive fear of adolescence – a fear which blurs thinking and alters social judgments – is the fear of rejection. Teens, like all minority groups who have no significance beyond the boundaries of their group, carry a certain panic about rejection because when rejected by their peers, they are pretty much nothing – and this is completely true in the teen culture. So much has been written about the adolescent's fear of rejection that I do not want to add to its volume here except to point out that rejection is not always a completely negative experience – even in the community of teens.

Ironically, for many teens rejection turns out to be a positive event in their social and moral development. To the delicate among you who believe that every rejection leaves an indelible scar on the teen's psyche, this, fortunately for all of us, is not the way it is.

One way to investigate this is to discuss teen rejection with young adults (which I have been doing on a regular basis for the past twenty years at the University of Alberta, and Okanagan University). With a surprising consistency young men and women tell stories about how their social bearings and their sense of direction were brought into sharper focus during early-adolescence after they had been rejected, or rebuffed, by some peer kingpin.

Rejection sets in motion a totally different set of mental operations than approval. The narcissistic benefits to *approval* are so convincing that intelligence is rarely used to investigate the reasons behind it. Rejection is a different matter; it insults deeply and must be explained. The adolescent's response to rejection may come in the form of denial or projection, but it may also come in the form of a reasoned and objective analysis – for most teens, it is a mixture of all of these.

The gain to this painful process is that adolescents begins to formalize a set of standards by which they evaluate not only the rejecting individual, the rejected behavior, but, rejection in general – its purposes, its motivations, who gains and who loses by it. These initial evaluations are a necessary first step in the attempt to understand the peer group, including its need to demote and promote, to humiliate and flatter. For many youngsters it marks the first cerebral distancing of self from the peer group, and leads to an awakening in their understanding of social life, namely that the peer group may reward or punish, and it may do so fairly or unfairly, and that it does not react only to "me," – it has its own life force, and its own need for survival. Attentive adults may perceive these insights as coming to know oneself, and in a way it is, but, as well, it is coming to know that neither peer acceptance nor peer rejection is the end of the social line. Adolescents do not make genuine progress with peer dominance until they recognize the inherent conflict between self and peers.

Rejection must be explained and explained in a way which creates less, not more, pain. The need to be protected from rejection triggers the adolescent's first serious analysis of human nature, or at least, teen nature. The results of this analysis go a long way toward determining how far the young person will bend to peer pressure. The more rejection is feared, the more the bending.

Emotional Utilitarianism in the Community of Teens

My friend, judge not me; Thou seest I judge not thee. (William Camden (1551-1623)

The conventions of the peer group, the pacts of friendship, and the oaths of love are given their authority by adolescent intelligence. The strengths of this intelligence are reflected in these rules, pacts, and oaths. It stands to reason, then, that we will learn something about teens when we understand how they determine who is a friend and who is a lover.

Our interest here is with three expressions of the psychodynamics of social survival. Each involves a coordinated perception in which two individuals enhance one another emotionally, and, at the same time, promote the friendship bond which unites them. In each instance a certain element of deception is involved, but the role this deception plays is so important to the survival of the friendship that neither partner acknowledges it. In our look at the psychodynamics of social survival, we will consider reciprocal rationalization, synchronized self-deception, and flattering mirrors. They each assume an important role in teen friendships. Let us begin, then, with how friendships are sustained by the belief of teens that it is their *duty* to bolster and defend their friends.

Reciprocal rationalization occurs when two people work cooperatively to reinforce and strengthen each other's rationalizations. In other words, instead of criticizing the fables and illusions of their partner, they reward them by pretending they are real. The cement is each partner's "duty" to honor the other, fables and all. While reciprocal rationalization allows one to passionately defend the friendship as true and authentic, it rarely is.

> "What I liked most was that he liked me." sixteen-year-old's response to the question: "What most attracted you to your first boyfriend?"

I have discovered in the course of hundreds of interviews that nineteen-twenty-two-year-olds quite freely admit that their early- and middle-adolescent friendships were largely self-serving and egoistic, and, furthermore, that reciprocal rationalization is part of the job description for most teen friendships, especially among younger teens. Rather than being embarrassed by this fact of their younger lives, most university students report matter-of-factly that such self-serving protectionism is simply part of growing up. Many of them view reciprocal rationalization as an unacceptable basis to friendship at their present maturity level, but as a somewhat inevitable fact of primitive bondings. Broadly speaking, I find myself in agreement with this assessment, because friendship during the early and middle teens tend to be utilitarian, situational, and exploratory. This generalization, though sweeping, is persistently accurate.

> He was older and more mature than friends my age – he was like a trophy for me. I found it very flattering for somebody in high school to want to be with somebody in jr. high. He even gave me his football jacket." First year university student's response to the question: "What most attracted you to your first boyfriend?"

Higher levels of human connection require common aims, loyalty, reasoned sacrifice for the partner, a willingness to help in a way that is needed, a respect for the partner as a person, and a clear awareness of where one stands in relation to the partner. Many adolescent bondings go by the name "friendship" because the partners spend so much time together and because they so desperately crave a loyal bond, but, at bottom, their bond is more need-driven than partner-driven, more self-centred than partner-centred. This is not to say that it is not friendship, indeed, for many youngsters it is the strongest bond they have ever known. This connection with another person, this bond of togetherness, is real but not what we would call genuine friendship. What then should we call it? The peer friendship of youth.

•   •   •

Teen friendships often have built into them a mutually enhancing arrangement where each person tacitly agrees not to notice certain undesirable things about the partner, and to preserve the deceit, and to make it more believable. The partners also agree not to notice that they do not notice. This psychic tap dance becomes a part of day-to-day life when friends, family members, and lovers learn to protect one another by failing to acknowledge certain buried secrets which, if uncovered, would force everyone to face hurtful and painful facts. Henrik Ibsen, the Norwegian dramatist and poet, called such buried secrets "vital lies" because they hide disturbing realities from conscious awareness. In teen society it is not advantageous to openly acknowledge the vices, defects or shortcomings of one's friends; indeed, it often is disastrous. Hence, synchronized silence carries with it a string of social rewards. Maintaining the silence is the first requirement of utilitarian friendship. On the other hand, with genuine friendship, unpleasant truths are examined honestly, with mutual encouragement, and a willingness to get to the heart of the matter even when it is painful to do so.

Synchronized self-deception permits each partner to develop a web of acceptable intrusions into the emotional life of the friend – intrusions which create emotionally charged connections while, at the same time, staying away from "out of bounds" domains of their friend's personality. These friendships forge an intense closeness with *part* of the person, and from this closeness a fractional intimacy is spun.

It helps to recognize the advantages of such an arrangement. Friends who honor the rule that certain questions must never to be asked in the presence of the protected person provide a certain measure of growing room where real strengths can be paraded while undeveloped qualities remain sequestered in the background. And, of course, synchronized self-deception protects the lesser side of one's nature from examination and disclosure.[3a]

•   •   •   •

A certain insight is gained when we observe friends who claim that they have *made up* after a quarrel (or disagreement, or difference of opinion), yet on close inspection we find that no real settlement of *the actual disagreement* has taken place at all. When reciprocal rationalization and synchronized self-deception permeate a relationship, *surviving* the disagreement is more important than the actual disagreement itself; "surviving" usually means that the partners have reassured each other, and that they admit to being sorry that they *hurt the feelings of the other*. The feelings of the partner are more important than the disagreement because the bond is more important than its substance, it is more important to repair the bond than the disagreement.

What really happens when friends claim they have "made up" is often word juggling and sentiment coddling more than problem solving. These same disagreements tend to arise again and again because their underlying causes are never addressed in a meaningful way. When partners claim that their disagreements have been worked out, they usually mean *that their alliance has been resumed.* The alliance holds because the real purpose of the friendship is emotional self-bolstering. Learning the differences between alliances grounded in self-bolstering and friendships grounded in mutual respect is part of what adolescence is all about. In this regard, friendship during adolescence is as much about learning as about feeling. It is, after all, the proving ground for intimacy and love.

Social Survival and Flattery

Sometimes we think we dislike flattery when it is only its method we dislike.
(de la Rochefoucauld)

Adolescents require friends who understand the world accurately and evaluate it honestly, who provide candid, evaluations, and who can discuss the disagreeable attributes of the friend. All of which is to say that they need reliable and honest friends to serve as *accurate mirrors*. This need, real as it is, does not always carry the day, and for a simple reason – an accurate mirror is often damaging to one's esteem. Accuracy has its place, but among the socially fearful it is not a place of very high standing.

A *flattering mirror*, on the other hand, reflects things as one wishes them to be, and this reflection can be comforting and uplifting to one's esteem. Many youngsters gain their social foothold simply by reflecting the pleasant and deflecting the unpleasant. This service is vital to the survival of all utilitarian relationships, and it is a service gladly provided by many, many kids in exchange for the short-term goodwill of their age mates.

Flattering mirrors become indispensable to the flattered one's sense of well-being. In these relationships praise is a duty of friendship. Praise and flattery are ends in themselves – their truth and their sincerity secondary to the emotional reassurance they bring. As flattery collusion continues each youngster takes an unspoken oath not to hurt or embarrass the other, and most certainly not to do anything which will lessen the other person's social worth. The unforeseen downside is that honest criticism comes to be regarded as an attack not only on the partner, but on the alliance as well.

> Because we believe our opinions are correct, we're not terribly suspicious of the motives of people who agree with us. (John Sabini)

Praise confirms to the hungry self that it is worthy. Praise – addicted youngsters may not know what they believe, but they do know that they crave being told again and again that they *truly* matter. This is the job of their flattering mirror, to remind their friends, again and again, of their greatness; all youth (except the completely dismissed) who excel at this honored responsibility are fully employed in the teen community.

To serve as a flattering mirror is not as easy as one might think. The flatterer must be able and to intuit the emotional requirements of the flattered one, and to recognize what is important at any given moment. The role of flattering mirror is a supportive one, and if Oscars were awarded in the adolescent theatre, flattering mirrors would compete for Best Supporting Actor and Best Supporting Actress. Their most prized skills are making the lead actor appear strong, central to the plot, and heroic, while remaining in the background, never stealing the scene.

All this is easier to comprehend when we recognize that one of the great experiences of adolescence is when someone is wild about you and will do anything for you, make any sacrifice to share your presence, to bask in your radiance. This is the narcissistic dream of every developing self. When you bring it to life, even briefly, you have grateful friends in the teen community.

To conclude this brief segment on flattering mirrors, I will leave you with a brief piece of rhetoric from the pen of Toni Morrison: "Could you really love somebody who was absolutely nobody without you? You really want somebody like that? Somebody who falls apart when you walk out the door?" This, of course, is three questions rather than one, but the answer to all three is the same when asked to the flattered one. And the answer is "Yes."

Concluding Comments

> They whose motive is utility have no real friendship for one another. (Aristotle)

Adolescent friendships can be a splendid and beautiful experience, but all friendships are not made of such stardust. This chapter has spoken almost exclusively to the less grand and less glorious aspects of adolescent relationships. Though this approach does not romanticize youth in the manner to which we have become unfairly accustomed, we do well to remind ourselves that when discussing something as fine as friendship there is no honor in denying its less noble elements.

Friendships rooted in reciprocal rationalization, synchronized self-deception, and flattering mirrors may eventually mature into relationships where truth and fairness are given greater play. However, they often do not for the simple reason that truth and fairness are not as highly valued in the teen world as approval and acceptance. This bitter truism is one we cannot overlook if we want to understand teen friendship.

In this chapter I have tried to explain how the following principles shape adolescent friendship.

• Young people are too insecure in their emotional core to completely and unreservedly share themselves with another person; hence, their relationships have a conditional, tentative, quality.

• Adolescents friendships are motivated as much by practical concerns and immediate needs as anything else; despite this utilitarian bent, friendships formed during the teen years may mature, into reciprocal, partner-driven relationships.

• The adolescent peer group, especially in the past four decades, has been contaminated by consumerism and the open display of brand names, and prestige clothing. (Prestige clothing is that which, for whatever reasons, bring peer praise, social acknowledgement, and the envy of others to its owner). I have intentionally avoided an analysis of this aspect of teen social survival to focus on the psychodynamics of adolescent social life. See [5, 6, 7] and the end of this chapter for further information on this topic.

• Not until the adolescent matures beyond utilitarian friendship, and has made forward progress in the identity project, is genuine intimacy, or love, possible.[8]

• Friendship helps young people to learn the ropes of their social system and to prepare for the more emotionally complex demands of intimacy and love.

• Adolescent friendships are grounded in both pragmatism and idealism, which is to say that they are intimate and instrumental, personal and practical, casual and intense. To see adolescent friendship as other-concerned (in contrast to self-concerned) is to completely misperceive its motivational dynamics.

• Adolescent friendship, especially in the beginning stages, often requires giving approval in exchange for approval being returned.

• Adolescent friendship often requires one friend to convince the other that his defects are virtues. This deception is not the pillar which supports all adolescent friendship, but it is a buttress without which many collapse.

Here we have looked at some of the demands behind social survival in the community of teens, keeping in mind that it is a community governed by a collective intellect which, for the most part, is juvenile in its operations and primitive in its morality. Like the corporate world, the community of teens has its tough side, and, also like the corporate world, if you don't learn to handle it, you soon are on the outside looking in.

Anecdotes and Supplemental Information

[1] **The survivalist quality of the teen community** is an important reason why we do not focus only on how adolescents *feel* about their friends. If feelings were the measure of friendship teen social life would be in much better shape than it is. To get to the heart of adolescent friendship we must also look at the motives which *impel, sustain,* and *dissolve* friendships.

[2] **The adolescent moratorium and the narrowness of teen life.** In North American culture, the time span covered by adolescence is also known as "the moratorium." Erik Erikson coined this term to mean a period of permissiveness between the juvenile incompetencies of childhood and the full responsibilities of adulthood; a delay of adult commitments characterized by a selective permissiveness on the part of society. The moratorium provides a protected period of experimentation to help young people become better able to assume personal obligations and to make meaningful commitments to their loved ones, and to their society. *Moratorium,* then, is the "in-between" world in which teens grow, mature, and prepare to meet the world.

The moratorium is defined by laws written and unwritten. The *written* laws require the parent society to provide basic health care, to educate, and to protect the young. The *unwritten* laws of the social contract claim that, in exchange for receiving food, shelter, emotional support, and schooling, the adolescent *should:* (a) remain in school until age 16, (b) avoid pregnancy, (c) avoid state-financed dependency, i.e., welfare, drug rehabilitation, prison, and, (d) work toward *acquiring* a mature identity. The major issues of adolescent life evolve around the adherence to, or the rejection of, these written and unwritten laws of the moratorium.

[3] **The analysis of teen friendships** is complicated by the fact that adolescents, especially early- and middle-adolescents, are not particularly skilled at appraising the human qualities of their friends.

In this chapter we have been addressing from a variety of angles a few basic questions: "Why are teens, under one set of circumstances, inclined to appraise their peers accurately, and, under another set of circumstances, inaccurately?" Parallel to this: "Why are teens, under one set of circumstances, inclined to appraise themselves accurately, and under another set of circumstances, inaccurately?" To assist in tackling these questions, B.B. Brown, M.S. Mory, and D. Kinney (1994) have assembled thoughtful ideas. Drawing upon principles of social identity theory, Brown, et al., claim that teens: (a) accentuate differences between their own group and other groups, (b) overstate the positive characteristics of their own group, and (c) overstate the negative characteristics of outside groups. These conclusions support general themes brought forward in Part I of this book, namely that the adolescent thought process is vulnerable to a host of interpretation biases which get in the way of a clear and objective understanding of themselves and their social world.

[3a]**Why do teens attribute moral profoundness to relationships which are essentially superficial?** Children, for example, do no such thing. One explanation is that the higher virtues of duty, honor, respect, and sacrifice are called upon to add dignity to a relationship which, in its particulars, doesn't have much of it. The frailty of the human connection is bolstered by the strength of the moral connection. This morality infusion is an unconscious attempt to enrich a friendship bond by bolstering it with moral imperatives. This same strategy is used by narcissists to make their relationships appear honest and fair when they are not.

[4]**Friendship patterns during early-, middle-, and late-adolescence**. As I have emphasized throughout this text, the differences in developmental maturity which take place between the beginning and the end of adolescence affect every aspect of life, including friendship and intimacy. Increased intellectual ability, and additional depth of feeling and breadth of morality contribute to an emotional-mental composition which is strikingly different. As one might anticipate, these differences shape not only friendship patterns, but the intellectual and moral perspectives which give them their meaning. Eastwood Atwater, (1998) explained some of these important differences this way:

> The meaning and quality of friendships tends to change throughout adolescence, most because of the developmental and social changes occurring during this period. Friendship gradually evolves from rather superficial, activity-oriented relationships in early-adolescence to more emotionally involved, intimate, and reciprocal relationships in late adolescence (p. 213)

For the most part, early-adolescent friendships are activity based, circumstance-driven, and even when they involve physical intimacy or sexual intercourse (as is increasingly common among early teens), they tend to lack depth of emotion and firmness of conviction. Self-disclosure, mutuality, and genuine concern for the partner are not nearly as important to younger teens as they will be in a few years.

During early-adolescence the residue of childhood flutters on the margins of desire, creating a child-like hue to their friendships; however, by mid-adolescence, their relationships are becoming more "adolescent," more emotional, more other-driven. Mid-adolescent friendships grow beyond the superficiality of early-adolescence without yet wading into the deeper emotional waters of late-adolescent intimacy.

> . . . friends of this age [mid-adolescence] engage in a great deal of self-disclosure, gossip, and the sharing of secrets. . . . Youths of this age are especially worried about friends talking about them behind their backs and failing to honor their secrets. Consequentl, mid-adolescent friendships tend to blow hot and cold, with sudden, dramatic changes and bitter feelings when friends break up (p. 215)

By late-adolescence, developmental progressions in mental maturity and moral outlook encourage greater self-disclosure, increased loyalty, and a greater desire for commitment.

[4a]**An easy way to envision the chronological progressions of early- middle- and late adolescence.**

From this alignment we see that early-adolescence overlaps childhood and adolescence, while late adolescence overlaps adolescence and early adulthood. This, in a nutshell, accounts for the mental and emotional differences between these two age groups .

⁵Material things and social survival in teen culture. The fable that everyone will admire every new purchase is the shared theme of all advertising. Youngsters who accept this illusion, even if they accept it only in part, soon find themselves locked into dependence on consumer goods not only for the approval these goods elicit from others, but for the approval they elicit from themselves because they are so hooked on material goods that without them self-approval is nearly impossible. The patchwork of reactions which make up the self-esteem network of adolescents (especially early- and middle-adolescents) is no match for the illusion industry. Teens are so hungry for approval that they willingly purchase what they think (or have been promised) will bring it. But, in consuming for emotional gain, they unknowingly makes themselves consumable objects as well.

Self-presentation rules teen life because so few teens hold a genuine sense of themselves, that they do not draw clear lines between (a) how they appear, (b) how they present themselves, and (c) how they *are*. (Indeed, during late childhood and early adolescence, many youngsters are completely stumped when they are asked to differentiate among the three.) In the early adolescent years, the self *must* be validated by others because it, quite literally, cannot validate itself; without the approval of others the self has no bearing, no direction. Approval is everything. The only force more powerful than approval is rejection.

Consumer frenzy among adolescents, when all is said and done, amounts to an insecure mind trying to decorate an unfinished body. Teens who bolster their social status with purchased goods soon discover that their dependency on image does not strengthen their sense of themselves, but weakens it through the fear that the goods they now own no longer work and must be continuously replaced with newer, more glittering goods.

CHILDHOOD	A D O L E S C E N C E	YOUNG ADULTHOOD

early-adolescence—middle-adolescence—-late-adolescence

Age   : 10, 11, 12, 13,   14,   15,   17, 18, 19, 20,   21

An all-too-frequent outcome is not an increase in esteem but an increase in envy; envy of those better able to purchase, and better able to display what they purchase. Ironically, what we see among teens is a hostile resentment of their possessions because of their dependence on them. Like the rest of us, teens cannot respect what they own when they do not first respect themselves.

⁶**Consumerism and the media: David Denby expressed it just right, "**. . . youth are shaped by the media as consumers before they have had a chance to develop their souls." The net effect is that teens are not only defenseless against the instinct

of acquisition which fetters human nature; they are programmed to glorify it before they have the intellectual maturity to examine it.

The mass media are the cornerstone of consumerism and perhaps more than any other force have embedded in the collective conscious of adolescents the belief that acceptance can be purchased.

> It is no coincidence that youths in North America are enthusiastic consumers of mass media products, such as magazines, movies, television, advertising, and music . . . "teenzines" (teen magazines directed at young women) report the latest news about fashion and music trends, and they link these with other youth-oriented, leisure industries through advertising . . . Almost one-half of the total magazine space was taken up by ads and that about one-half of these ads were selling beauty-care products, fashion, clothing, and other items designed to enhance young women's appearance and popularity. (Cote & Allahar, p. 89-90)

[7]**More consumerism and the media.** David Denby (July 15, '96 *The New Yorker)* spoke of the "avalanche of crud" which drowns adolescents in our consumer-driven culture. Individual instances, he claims, cannot convey its subversive power; but its collective impact allows us to see it for what it is.

> Even if the child's character is not formed by a single TV show, movie, or video or computer game, the endless electronic assault obviously leaves its mark all over him . . . Whether the sets are on or off, the cruddy tone is on the air and in the streets. The kids pick it up and repeat it, and every week there are moments when I feel the spasm of fury that surges back and forth between resentment and self-contempt . . . The crude bottom-line attitude they've picked up, the nutty obsessive profanity, the echo chambers of voices and attitudes, set my teeth on edge . . . What American parent hasn't felt that spasm? Your kid is rude and surly and sees everything in terms of winning or losing or popularity and becomes insanely interested in clothes and seems, far, far from courage and selfhood.

> Aided by armies of psychologists and market researchers, the culture industries reach my children at every stage of their desires and their inevitable discontent . . . In this country people possessed solely by the desire to sell have become far more powerful than parents . . .

We might add, more powerful than the younger adolescents they target.

[8]**Adolescent friendship and adolescent love.** At the risk of racing ahead of the scheduled flow of ideas, it is helpful to point out here that the emotional and mental features of the adolescent personality which constrain the possibilities of friendship also exert a dampening effect on the prospects for love. Love is not out of the question, but it is a terrific challenge for the adolescent mental and emotional fabric. We will delve further into the developmental preconditions of mature love in Chapters Eleven and Twelve.

Eleven

The Search for Intimacy

In order to establish intimate relations with others, one must first know who and what one is. (Jerome Dusek)

Almost a century after G. Stanley Hall, North America's first great adolescent psychologist, wrote: "As to the sentiment of love in the adolescent, we still know too little." We remain pretty much in the dark concerning the causes, the origins, and the expressions of adolescent love. This is not a good state of affairs, as right now adolescent love, or at least what passes for it in the teen community, is among the most significant issues in the health and well-being of youth in North American culture.

Before we may proceed with this topic we need to recognize our limitations. First, there is no genuine agreement among psychologists, or any other group of "youth experts," as to the meaning of "love" or "adolescent love." The prevailing attitude of this book is that adolescents, especially early- and middle-adolescents, are lacking in key developmental progressions required of "mature love," most notably their underdeveloped and incomplete identity. Further, adolescents are constrained by a thought process vulnerable to misperception and miscomprehension when dealing with emotionally charged issues such as love or intimacy. Adolescents themselves are highly confused about intimacy; they define it, express it, and experience it in profoundly diverse ways. So, it is presumptuous for psychologists to have a clarity about intimacy which those who experience it do not.

To get around the inherent vagaries of the meaning of "love," and to avoid the heat which the word itself creates, in this chapter we refer to "adolescent intimacy," rather than to "adolescent love." This does not solve the problem, as "intimacy" also, defies neat and tidy summary, but it seems to me that intimacy is easier to handle than love.

Adolescent intimacy is a necessary area of inquiry in the emotional life of youth. It is far deeper, and carries greater consequences, than other expressions of teen friendship. Intimacy differs from friendship in the depth of its feeling, in the power of its conviction, in its concern for the *real* needs of the partner, and its romantic and sexual elements.

A tight definition of intimacy is almost impossible, but Harry Stack Sullivan's, penned a half century ago, holds up better than most. "Intimacy requires a clearly formulated adjustment of one's behavior *to the expressed needs of the other person* in the pursuit of increasingly identical – *that is more and more nearly mutual satisfactions*" (1953, p. 246). I have emphasized two phrases in this well known quote to draw attention to *genuine* needs and *mutual* satisfactions. Intimacy requires care, respect, and responsiveness to the partner's growth and happiness; and, by implication, it requires the *maturity of selfhood* to recognize the partner's real needs, and the *maturity of thought* to think evenly about, and act directly upon, the partner's best interests. Intimacy is grounded in *genuine* concern for the partner, in mutual admiration and honest reciprocity. For most adolescents this is a tough set of requirements to meet; for many it is impossible.

During adolescence intimacy is easily confused with infatuation, superficial attraction, erotic fascination, and need gratification. Part of the sorting out process of adolescence is learning to recognize intimacy for what it is, and to separate it from its lesser impersonations, and it is only fair to report that some adolescents are far better than others at this.[1]

Know Thyself – Intimacy and Self-Definition

Before entering on the subject of the adolescent's search for intimacy, I must make a few preliminary comments. First, the search for intimacy is tightly bound with the quest for identity – also known as the "identity project." As youth become more sophisticated in their self-knowledge and more purposeful in their life direction, the desire for a partner with whom to share oneself also grows. Typically, as adolescents move into young adulthood they are not only more capable of intimacy and love, but they are more desirous of it. Second, the desire for intimacy does mean that the individual has a mature identity. (Indeed, some teens who most desire intimacy are least able to handle its demands on their identity.) Thus, before we can discuss intimacy we need to spend a moment discussing identity.

Is mature identity necessary before one can experience genuine intimacy? This is the primary question in every theory of adolescent intimacy. The fact that virtually no one has provided a satisfactory answer doesn't detract from its importance.

Adolescent identity has been the object of systematic investigation for more than fifty years, having been introduced by Erik Erikson in his landmark essay "Ego development and historical change" in 1946. Since his pioneer efforts, most psychologists have come to accept that young people achieve identity as they invest themselves in a relatively stable set of values and beliefs, and as they formulate a set of career goals and occupational options.

Identity includes the loving and sharing, as well as the shameful and punitive, elements of our nature. Identity means an integration of all previous identifications and self images, including the negative ones. Therefore, when we discuss identity we recognize the continuity of identity despite changes taking place within it, a unique differentiation from all other people, the essential character which resides within a given individual, and that identity requires effort and purposeful direction, which is to say that youth must work on becoming who they are, they must expend energy to become more than who they are.

Identity is not finalized during adolescence, nor does any valid reason indicate that it should be. Adolescence, however, is the age when identity assumes its adult outlines, and when it attains the strength and autonomy we associate with the adult character.

In sum, healthy identity includes (1) an honest recognition of one's strengths and weaknesses, (2) a fairly solid sense of family and community, (3) a stable set of beliefs by which to make *important* decisions, and (4) a belief in one's ability to cope with adversity. Identity is a major life accomplishment, and while much of it is constructed during adolescence, it continues to grow and evolve throughout the adult years. After all, what do we think of a fifty-year-old who has the identity development of an eighteen-year-old!

Now to the question at hand: "Are adolescents mature enough in their identity for intimacy?"

It is my belief that a solid sense of identity is a requirement for mature intimacy; after all, it is one's identity which is shared in intimacy, and one cannot share what one does not have. As Erik Erikson expressed it: "It is only when identity formation is well on its way that true intimacy . . . is possible" (1968, p. 135). In other words, intimacy cannot come into being until certain preconditions have been met. Here is another way to look at it.

> In order to establish intimate relations with others, one must first know who and what one is. . . . If one is to reveal the inner self to others, one must know what the inner self is and have self-acceptance; for if one cannot accept the self, how can one ask others to accept it? (Dusek, 1991, p. 152)

Teens hit a major roadblock when the intimacy project becomes more important than the identity project. In other words, when they invest more time and energy securing an intimacy partner than in building the self-knowledge, strength of character, and life purpose required to sustain intimacy. This phenomenon, and it is not a rare one, means that young people embrace intimacy's possibilities before they can handle its realities, a propensity which holds staggering consequences for the teen community and even more for the adult community which nurtures and subsidizes it. We do not exaggerate with the claim that early- and mid-adolescents meet their greatest life crises when they secure an intimacy partner before their identity can cope with the emotional demands of intimacy.

Teens bond, pledge their loyalty, and share their emotions – the behavior of intimacy. These emotion-charged experiences may be perceived by teens as *love*, however, love is rarely what it is. Powerful feelings are essential to love, but unto themselves are not love. No matter how intense, erotic, and sincere the connection may be, without an awareness of the partner as person, it is not love that blooms. It is rich, it is real, it is more profound than anything which comes before it. Is it love? Not really. What then? *Adolescent* intimacy.

The point to be grasped here is elementary, but its implications are immense: because their identities are in process, and because their self-knowledge is in flux, adolescents have great difficulty balancing the rightful needs of the self with the rightful needs of their partner. The egocentrism which shapes the personality makes it difficult for them to perceive their partner's real needs, and the narcissism which shapes their behavior makes it difficult for them to effectively gratify these needs. In sum, few adolescents are emotionally or mentally able to meet the demands of mature intimacy.

Primitive Intimacy

It is my observation that many psychologists make the same mistake that adolescents themselves make when it comes to intimacy: they fail to distinguish between its primitive and mature expressions. Teens, and far too many teen experts, share the myth that intimacy is *natural* to adolescence when, in fact, it is not. The desire for intimacy, and the search for intimacy, are nearly universal, but the attainment of it is a rarity.

As part of my research with adolescents I have interviewed many twelve-fifteen-year-olds who are pregnant, or who have recently given birth. Many of these girls (I have trouble calling them "young women" even though their life-experience justifies it) tell stories of special relevance to the questions we are looking at. It is not unusual to meet a young mother who refuses to talk to the man (boy) who fathered her child because she feels betrayed.[3, 4] The stories these girls tell hold a surprising consistency. The boy is often three or four years older (during early- or middle-adolescence this amounts to a tremendous psycho-emotional advantage). At the beginning of the relationship the boy praises, pursues, and woos the girl with an earnest aggressiveness. The girls perceive the boy's actions as proof that he is in "love" (sometimes these girls believe that the actions, unto themselves, *are* love). The girl accepts the boy's persistence as a singular interest in her, and as proof of her desirability, even when she has been forewarned by her girl friends, her mother, and sometimes, even the boy's friends. Their involvement becomes sexual, she becomes pregnant, he becomes gone. She feels betrayed; she trusted him and he turned out to be fraudulent. Her betrayal transforms into shame, then anger, then ongoing resentment. Yet open condemnation of the boy destroys her value as the object of his love; to lessen him is to lessen herself. A tough call for a youngster struggling to hold on to even a minimal sense of her own worth as a person, but also, as a recipient of another's love.

> *He liked me; he paid attention to me; he was cool; he was a show off; he was cute.* A fifteen-year-old girl's response to the question: What most attracted you to the first guy you had sexual intercourse with?

The deception is a two-way street. The girl cannot distance herself from the praise, the chase, the eroticism. These girls discredit their own reality checks (a common practice among early-adolescents). At a certain level they know that love is not what is happening, but knowing does not prevent hoping. The young mother, while deploring her mate's desertion, also sings his praises, first and foremost of which was his "love" for her.

A fifteen-year-old mother in rural Washington described the adolescent father of her child this way: "He was a liar most of the time, but he made me feel good. He was always nice to me so I can't be too mad at him." Her best girl friend, age sixteen, also has a baby. Of the father of her child she said: "I'm glad I didn't have to marry him but I wouldn't want to have never met him. He was a nice guy, just not dependable. I kinda thought this [becoming a mother] might happen, but I never thought much about it." A seventeen-year-old from Portland, Oregon offered this: "I liked it when he was nice to me. I don't know if I ever *loved* him, even though I told everyone I did. I just liked his always wanting to do things for me, and his always saying nice things to me."[5, 6]

This is the intimacy typical of teen relationships – intimacy nourished by affective logic, by personal fables, by the need to give oneself, by the desire to bond, by particularization, and by the need to be admired and loved.

Infatuation. Infatuation is a state of attraction where one is preoccupied with the partner so fully that thoughts and feelings about them intrude involuntarily into consciousness, and where other concerns recede into the background, where one longs to be with the partner, where one has an acute sensitivity to the reactions of the partner, where one feels buoyant, vitalized, and swept away, and, where one is obsessed with the admirable traits of the partner. Infatuation is intense, passionate, and short-lived. Adolescents, especially early- and middle-teens, confuse it with love; a confusion which derives from their tendency to overvalue the significance of self-arousal, and to overrate the profundity of self-experience. Their thinking operates on the premise that the greater my experience, the greater am I. It is doubly reinforcing; I am great, therefore, so are my experiences; my experiences are great, therefore, so am I. Narcissistic logic, to be sure, but during a time of life when one struggles to connect inner-feeling with outer-reality, it is a compelling logic.

How does infatuation differ from mature intimacy? From love? Generally speaking, infatuation is triggered by superficial features rather than substantive ones, grounded in physicality more than in caring, one-sided rather than reciprocal, stagnant rather than growth-fostering, and, ". . . pervaded with illusion rather than honest attempts at mutual understanding" (Martin, 1996, p. 13). In sum, infatuation is a brush with intimacy but not intimacy itself. It is wrong to trivialize it, but it is preposterous to idealize it, overvalue it, or pretend that it is mature intimacy.

Infatuation can be a cruel introduction to intimacy since it rarely lives up to expectations. While infatuation may, in the course of time and togetherness, lead to intimacy, it cannot without growing beyond itself. What then is infatuation? Primitive intimacy.

The language of intimacy. When speaking with adolescents about intimacy (interestingly, they rarely use this word in ordinary conversation), one cannot help but be struck by their fascination with the pronoun "I." This is due partly to their lack of skills in explicit communication, and partly to their nervous self-consciousness, but whichever plays the greater role, it conveys the insecurity in which youthful intimacy is grounded. Adolescent intimacy is beckoned by mutuality, but it is grounded in individuality.

When listening to teens talk about their relationships one gets the feeling that each partner has sculpted a patch of identity turf and, having done so, sends out feeler invitations for someone to come in and share it. These invitations are a necessary prelude to intimacy, and a first step in forming a love relationship, but unto themselves, they are neither.

He was charming; a sweet talker. I was attracted to him because he thought I was hot. He treated me nice." An eighteen-year-old response to the question: "What attracted you to the first boy you had intercourse with?"

Despite being embroiled within it, teens are not very good at expressing deep emotion. But their difficulties are multiplied a dozen fold when they try to express it to someone who is listening intently to every word they say, and who holds a charged interest in exactly how they say it. This inclines them to communicate the power of their affection through touch, closeness, fidelity, and possessiveness more than through words, phrases, sentences, and paragraphs. Teens feel the power, the eroticism, the highs and lows of intimacy, but without a language to effectively express these feelings.

Intimate language is an art form which requires self-knowledge, self-esteem, and a certain clarity about which emotions one is actually experiencing. It is virtually impossible for those weak in self-knowledge, low in self-esteem, and uncertain about which emotions they are feeling at any given instant.

Sharing in the pleasure of the partner. Mature intimacy requires concern for the *genuine* needs and the *real* feelings of the partner. Brehm, in her excellent work on human relationships, spoke to this issue: "In close, rewarding, intimate relationships, partners will meet each other's needs, disclosing feelings and sharing confidences, discussing practical concerns, helping each other, and providing reassurance" (1991). Many teens struggle with this condition of intimacy because their over-riding self-consciousness makes impossible the free and open sharing in the pleasures of their partner. Indeed, pleasure within the partner often produces envy and jealousy rather than joy and pride.

It would be unfair to claim that adolescents do not share in the pleasures of their partners. The problem comes when the pleasure occurs in an arena where one of the partners is excluded. Pleasure which is experienced *outside the circumference of the partnership* produces a tightness in the chest more than joy in the soul. Why? Adolescents are confused as to how another person can bring pleasure to their loved one. Their narcissistic perceptions cause them to believe that only they can bring deep pleasure to their partner. When they see their partner enjoying themselves it makes them feel replaceable. The "left out" partner counter-attacks with an ultimatum: there will be no outside pleasures.

The action of intimacy. Mature intimacy is felt in the heart, but expressed in action. The action of intimacy, not the emotion of intimacy, distinguishes the primitive from the mature expression. Primitive intimacy is grounded in feeling – this it shares with mature intimacy. The difference is that mature intimacy is followed up with partner-affirming action. Mature intimacy expresses itself in the action of *giving* oneself in affirming ways; in *caring* for the needs and eccentricities of the partner; in *responsibility* to the partner's best interests; in *respect* for the integrity of the partner; in *understanding* the individuality of the partner. As youth participate in these *acts of intimacy,* they move toward intimacy, and toward love. All of which takes us back to Shakespeare: "They do not love that do not show they love."

Creating the Perfect Partner

Our judgments concerning the worth of things depend on the feelings the things arouse in us. (William James)

James' message is simple but profound: as our feelings increase in power so also do our *judgments* about the people associated with them. This phenomenon I call "particularization."

Particularization is the belief that the person with whom we share a love experience is the cause of that experience; and, further, that without this *particular person,* the love experience could never be. Rather than attribute love to themselves, (that is, their inner feelings, their warmth, their sexuality), the experience is attributed entirely to the partner. One result of this attribution is that the partner attains a splendor (and a power) beyond anything known in ordinary friendships.

Love, after all, is directed to a particular individual; it *is* particular. Love finds a singular, unique particularity in the lover. The French writer Stendhal claimed "lovers endow their partners with a thousand perfections, and draw from every event proof of the perfection of the loved one."

Adolescents are excited by the idea that their love is nurtured by a particular, super-special person. The young, as often is true for the elderly, readily believe that only one person can create love and when that person is gone so also is love. This is the reasoning of particularization.

When love is experienced with only one particular person that experience may attain life-and-death urgency. When the lover is lost, an overpowering loss descends, for in losing the person one has forever lost love, or so it appears. When the "my love is more profound than all other love" fable enters, the stage is set for the adolescent's willingness to make any sacrifice for the beloved partner.

A tragic example of particularization:

A HUMAN TRAGEDY
TEENAGE LOVERS COMMIT SUICIDE

Sweetwater, Florida (AP)-The bodies of two teenagers were found floating in a canal Tuesday in what police say was a case of a couple who preferred death to being forbidden to see each other.

Police believe the bodies were those of 13-year-old Maryling and 14-year-old Christian, missing since Sunday. Pending autopsies, the bodies were not positively identified.

The teens appeared to have taken their own lives, like Romeo and Juliet in Shakespeare's play about forbidden love, said Sweetwater Det. Ramon Quintero. Both left suicide notes.

"We don't suspect any foul play," Quintero said. "The mother of the girl did not want the boy seeing her daughter. It is very sad."

Family members told police the teens – both honor students at Ruben Dario middle school in northwest Dade County – ran away early Sunday, carrying little money and no extra clothes.

"The children probably drowned themselves", said Quintero, a friend of the girl's family. "Neither knew how to swim.

Christian, fourteen, left this note in his bedroom:

To everyone:

I can't go on living. I've lost Maryling. That's something that hurts me very deep inside of my heart. I'll remember all of you. None of you will be forgotten. Please don't forget me. I love all of you. I've put my best these 14 years I've been on this hellhole called Earth. I bid farewell to all. Please keep me in your hearts, because I know all of you will be in mine.

I am not leaving you, I'm escaping from the realm of reality into the darkness of the unknown. Because reality is, I can't be with Maryling, and even the strongest man in the world wouldn't resist the loss of a loved one that was held so near and dear to your heart.

Nothing can stop me now. I'm taking my life because without Maryling, I have no life. Funny . . . Karen was talking about suicide earlier. I never thought it would have anything to do with me. So, say farewell to all. And as the immortal Beethoven once said: "Applaud, friends, the comedy is over." I leave you with the same words.

I love you all,

Christian

Maryling, 13, left this note to her parents:

Mom and Dad:

You'll never be able to understand the love between me and Christian. I feel that without him I can't live. Why is it you were never able to understand me? Or is it that you live to make my life miserable? I love him more than anyone here on this Earth. I'll never be happy without him.

You don't let me see him in this world, so we're going to another place.

I love you all very much. I'd like to ask for your forgiveness, but I know you will never understand me. This is all I want to tell you: I love him and I will always love him very much. But I will never be able to stay on this Earth without him.

Please don't cry for me, this is what I want. I want to feel happy, because right now I'm going to a place where I can be with Christian. Lastly, I'm sorry that I couldn't be with you all.

I love you all very much,

Maryling

Fable and Illusion in Adolescent Intimacy

> Illusions serve love by strengthening attraction through exaggerating the positive and downplaying the negative features of the beloved. (Mike W. Martin)

I do not want to make the case that adolescent love is delusional (as did Schopenhauer and Freud), but I do want to make clear that it is characterized by delusional qualities. In making the case that adolescent love is a primitive expression of love, I am not advancing the "pathology-passing-for-love" point of view so popular today, nor am I trying to promote the idea of "addictive love" which clutters bookstore shelves. I am merely trying to describe adolescent love for what it is.

Like all self-serving beliefs, particularization is, at bottom, an attempt to elevate the self by the glorifying self-experience. Particularization bestows the partner with qualities worthy of true love and total commitment; a person greater than "I" and, greater than "I" deserve. (And, what *is* better than to be loved by someone greater than oneself?)[7]

A simple principle is at work here: when we elevate someone we love, we elevate ourselves. Perhaps nowhere is this principle more clearly demonstrated than in the romantic relationships of early adolescent girls. Not unfailingly, but with remarkable consistency, they view their boyfriends as more committed to them than they are, more in love than they are, more virtuous than they are, and more talented than they are. These girls may hold accurate perceptions *in general* but when it comes to their "love" and their "relationship," they often are so amiss as to be illusional. But the illusion is everything. Susan Moore and Doreen Rosenthal provide interesting background on this issue:

> We found that young women were more likely to define their sexual encounters as occurring with a regular or steady partner than with a casual partner, while young men were more likely to regard what must be essentially the same encounters as casual . . . in fact the male interpretation of what is going on may be closer to reality. The girls are interpreting, as an indication of love and commitment, encounters which often turn out to be short-term. (1994, p. 98)

Lauren Ayers, in her thoughtful and sensitive work, *Teenage Girls,* claimed "teenagers are not able, as a rule, to be mature and responsible about sexual relating" (1994, p. 164). Her statement, assuming its essential correctness, (which I do), deserves our full attention since in today's culture about one half of *all* teen-age girls are involved in sexual relationships, and about 20% of them become pregnant during their teen years.

Final Comments on the Adolescent Quest for Intimacy

> The desire for intimacy acts as love's advance guard. (Jose Ortega Y Gasset)

In this chapter we have considered the idea that early and middle-adolescents are not emotionally ready for intimacy or love. More specifically, their beliefs about their partners are shaped by particularization, and the intellect which guides their search for intimacy is swayed by narcissistic cravings and motive mis-perception. My point of view on this topic is, I believe, well supported by developmental theory and psychological research. But even if it were not, we would still be left with the evidence of our experience which teaches us that early teens simply do not have the maturity of identity nor the emotional continuity required of genuine intimacy. The issue is a serious one because, for most teens, intimacy is the precursor to sexual intercourse, sexual intercourse to pregnancy, and pregnancy to the depletion of human capital in the adolescent community. Pregnancy is the number one at-risk behavior for teens in North American culture.

In its optimal expression, intimacy is partner fusion characterized by mutuality, honest communication, and emotional commitment. In its primitive expression it is partner fusion characterized by elevated self-awareness, honest monologue, and emotionalism. On the surface, these differences may not appear significant, indeed many teens don't seem to recognize them at all, but in their day-to-day implications they are profound.

It is unfair to suggest that intimacy is *never* experienced during adolescence; but during early- and middle-adolescence it is extremely rare. At this age teens are simply too involved in the legitimate demands of their own growth and development to draw clear distinctions between their own needs and yearnings and the needs and yearnings of their partner. This, as far as intimacy is concerned, is a big problem.

Anecdotes and Supplemental Information

[1] **Definition of intimacy.** I have not put forth a scientific definition of intimacy because the word defies a brief, workable definition. Karen Prager, in her superb book, *The Psychology of Intimacy*, spent the entire first chapter trying to do so, and eventually surrendered. But she did point out something worth a moment of our time. She writes: "Ideally, a definition [of intimacy] scholars use should be reconcilable with lay definitions. A scholarly definition clearly needs more precision than do lay definitions, but it may not be useful if it excludes many of the experiences the average layperson would call intimate. The risk of deviating too much from lay definitions is that research will be undertaken that has little relevance to people's everyday experiences with intimacy" (1995, p. 14). With this statement I am in complete agreement.

[2] **Intimate relationships** exist on many planes. In terms of *intensity*, some intimate relationships are intense while others are calm and tranquil. In terms of *commitment*, some relationships are sealed by a commitment to longevity while others are brief. In terms of *emotion*, feelings run the gamut from ecstatic joy to agonizing despair. In terms of *sexuality*, some are erotic and sexual, some not. In terms of gender, men and women (as well as boys and girls) often take different approaches to intimacy. Intimate relationships may exist between same-sex partners and between partners of the opposite sex (Brehm, 1992).

[3]**Pregnancy during adolescence.** Even though we know the incidence of sexual behavior at virtually every developmental level, we have no clear understanding *why* teens are so inept at avoiding pregnancy. Nor do we understand why teens cling to irrational beliefs about pregnancy – especially the "It can never happen to me" fable.

Mothers under age fifteen experience a rate of maternal deaths two and one half times that of mothers aged twenty to twenty-four. Teen mothers also have a higher rate of nonfatal complications than non-teen mothers; the younger the mother the higher the risk for such complications of pregnancy as toxemia, anemia, prolonged labor, and premature labor; teen mothers are 92% more likely to have anemia, 23% more likely to experience premature birth than mothers in their twenties. Teenage pregnancies more frequently end in miscarriage and stillbirths than pregnancies of women in their 20s. Babies born to teenagers are more likely to be premature, to have low birth weights, to have low Apgar scores, and to die within the first month and within the first year. Low birth weight contributes to cerebral palsy, mental retardation, epilepsy, and is a major cause of infant mortality. The Carnegie Council on Adolescent Development (1989) reports that medical costs for low-birth weight infants average $400 000. (By the time you read these figures they will be much higher).

[4]**Men, boys, and teen pregnancy.** The choice of "man" rather than "boy" is a real one in the case of teen pregnancy. Most research confirms that more than 50% of babies born to teens are fathered by adults.

[5]**Why can't teens avoid pregnancy?** A reproof to those who think of adolescents as masters of their own destiny is that they have such extreme difficulty avoiding pregnancy. Yet, in a few short years, with the onset of early adulthood, they have no such difficulty at all. The "pregnancy pockets" of middle and late adolescence are, for all intents and purposes, a thing of the past by the early twenties. Girls who avoid pregnancy during the critical years of fifteen to eighteen, rarely experience unwanted pregnancies during later years.

[6]**The adult years following teen pregnancy.** The impact of teen motherhood was effectively summarized by Arthur Campbell:

> The girl who has an illegitimate child at the age of sixteen suddenly has ninety percent of her life script written for her. She will probably drop out of school; even if someone else in her family helps to take care of the baby, she will probably not be able to find a steady job that pays enough to provide for herself and her child; she may feel impelled to marry someone she might not otherwise have chosen. Her life choices are few, and most of them are bad. (From Ginzberg et al., 1988)

By age 29 about 50% of women who had their first child as a teen had obtained a high school diploma, while over 95% of those who did not have their first child until after age 20 had obtained a high school diploma. Mothers without a high school diploma are twice as likely to live in households receiving Aid to Families with Dependent Children. Women whose first child was born in their adolescence produce more children in their lifetime than women whose first child was born after adolescence.

Teenage mothers pose a substantial cost to the state. "A major source of new applications/acceptance on welfare rolls is the young teenage mother who, in the absence of a wage-earning male, frequently has no other source of income to cover living expenses for her child and herself." A significant factor for teen mothers is longevity: "Although many adults who go onto the rolls leave within a relatively brief time (less than two years), many teenage mothers remain for a decade if not longer" (Ginzberg et al., p. 30).

[7]**"Fame by association"** works two ways. The first is seen when the young person finds someone acknowledged by peers, society, or tradition to be great, and then affixes himself (herself) to this great person. The second is when the young person first affixes to someone and afterward creates a network of justifications (some contrived, some real) which prove that this person *is* great.

[8]**Fear of intimacy.** In this chapter we have neglected an important phenomenon – the fear of intimacy. Our neglect is due to the fact that our primary concern has been the adolescent's readiness (or lack of readiness) for intimacy and love. Nevertheless, the fear of intimacy is an issue worth looking at in our attempt to understand the dynamics of adolescent behavior.

Intimacy often triggers pre-existing personality weaknesses within one or both of the partners, which may have gone unnoticed during previous conditions of casual friendship or pseudo-intimacy. Therefore, intimacy partners not only encounter the stress of adjusting to one another, they must also come to grips with deficiencies within their own personality. Intimacy brings joyous connections but it also exposes the dark side of the personality; hence, it involves both pleasure and pain, a mixture many teens would rather avoid altogether.

Twelve

Echo Love

Lovers accentuate their beloved's good qualities and downplay their flaws. In that process they are notoriously prone to illusions and self deceptions. (Mike W. Martin)

At this moment those of us who write about adolescent love don't know enough even to decide if it originates in the sexual impulse, as was first argued by Socrates and later by Schopenhauer and then by Freud. We so-called "authorities" on adolescent love are in a position of "ignorant expertise," as Gordon Allport liked to phrase the condition, where experts know more and more about less and less. Amidst all this confusion, I have come to believe that most experts on adolescent love miss the boat altogether because most of what passes for love during adolescence is not love at all. In this chapter I will try to explain why I think this way; it begins with a look at Narcissus and Echo, Ovid's ancient symbols of youthful love.

The Echo Legend

Narcissus was a beautiful young man of mythological antiquity who took love, but did not give it in return. His self-absorption and self-fascination was so great that his name is now a synonym for impenetrable vanity. He left in his wake the broken hearts and crushed spirits of all those who loved him; for their love they received only the emptiness and the pain of love unreciprocated. The Narcissus of yesterday, like the narcissists of today named after him, was unworthy of the love showered upon him.

Narcissus is of interest to us for many reasons, foremost being that his relentless self-obsession did not keep lovers at their distance; indeed, they fell before him like roses before a returning conqueror. Those who pursued him, and there were many, kept up their pursuit even though he never surrendered to it. Indeed, they were attracted to the very self-absorption which cancelled their own value as lovers and as people. We now come to Echo, who was the deepest suffering and most tormented of all those who tried vainly to capture Narcissus' love. Herself an adolescent, Echo idolized her distant hero, believing to the end that this beautiful, intelligent boy would one day fall out of fascination with himself and into love with her. Of course, he did not.

Legend tells us that Echo was a beautiful nymph, fond of the woods and the hills. One day she saw beautiful Narcissus hunting in the hills. She hurriedly followed his footsteps. How she longed to address him in the softest accents, and win him to conversation. But it was not in her power. She, therefore, waited with impatience for him to speak first, and had her answer ready. One day Narcissus, being separated from his companions, shouted aloud, "Who's here?" Echo replied in the only way she could, "Here." Narcissus looked around, but seeing no one called out, "Come." Echo answered, "Come." As no one came Narcissus called again, "Why do you shun me?" Echo then asked the same question. "Let us join one another," said the beautiful youth. Echo answered with all her heart in the same words, and hastened to the spot, ready to throw her arms about his neck. But he turned away in anger and disgust. "Not so," he said; "I will die before I give you power over me." All that Echo could say was, humbly, entreatingly, "I give you power over me," but he was gone. She hid her blushes and her shame in a lonely cave, and never could be comforted. Yet, still her love remained firmly rooted in her heart, and was increased by the pain of having been rejected. Her anxious thoughts kept her awake and made her pitifully thin. They say she has so wasted away with longing that only her voice now is left to her.

At last one of those he wounded said a prayer and it was answered by the gods: "May he who loves not others love himself." The goddess of righteous anger, Nemesis, undertook to bring this about. As Narcissus bent over a clear pool and saw his own reflection he fell in love. In that instant of mesmerized self-fascination his fate was sealed; and like all narcissists to follow him, his self-obsession destroyed his connection to all other selves, even of hopeful lovers.

Echo yearned for Narcissus even after he time and again rejected her, and she did so without even a moment of closeness with him, without the comfort of his touch or caress, and with complete awareness that Narcissus neglected everyone who desired him. Why Echo burned with desire for Narcissus, and wanted nothing more than to be by his side when he showed no interest in her, is an unsolved mystery (which is part of the myth's allure) but there can be no doubt that, at least by modern standards, Echo's love was grounded in an inner emptiness which she desperately hoped Narcissus would lovingly fill. Her relentless pursuit proved to Narcissus his power over her. Rejected and abandoned, Echo withered away, mythology's first anorexic; she starved from unreciprocated love, a love which she valorized until the moment of her death. (Like so many of her adolescent sisters of today, Echo could not differentiate obsession from love.) The story of Echo is one of self-love and self-denial; a story of a young woman who knew nothing of love except its pain and rejection. There was no awareness from either partner of the humanity or the personhood of the other. Narcissus and Echo shared no real communication, no genuine awareness or open concern for the human needs of the other. This is not a love story. It is the tragedy of a young woman, really a teen-age girl, driven by the desire for love but without enough self-knowledge, or knowledge of love itself, to see her obsession for what it was. She valorized her illusions to the moment of her death, but tragic as her obsession was, there was no real love in it.

We simplify unfairly when we believe that Echo was drawn to Narcissus only by his beauty, although beauty certainly hurried things along. Echo was consumed with the illusion that Narcissus' love would fill her emptiness. The pathos of Narcissus was his inability to invest in anything outside of himself; the pathos of Echo was her willingness to give herself to a man incapable of love, to then deny that his love for himself was greater than his love for her. Echo "loved" to her death a young man who, by every dignified standard, was unworthy of her love.

Echo's obsession with Narcissus is viewed by some as misdirected love and by others as a spiritual deficiency; here (since our focus is on adolescence, and since Echo herself was younger even than Narcissus) her tragedy is not viewed as love at all, but as one expression of immature, obsessive love, Echo love.[1]

What, after all, did Echo really think she was doing when she put her destiny in the hands of a sixteen-year-old boy whose notable qualities (other than beauty) were selfishness and vanity? Or was she thinking at all? (By now, we recognize that this is no mere idle question.) Was she so love struck that she could not see him for what he was? Was she so devoid of vision that she could not foresee the outcome to their coupling? Was there something seductive about Narcissus' boundless self-absorption? Was Echo really a woman, or only a child in a woman's body?

We, of course, do not know the answer to any of these questions, nor can we ever know. But we are concerned with Echo's love for Narcissus because her self-destructive actions ring as true today as yesterday; we also are concerned with Narcissus because the selfish obsessions, the imperviousness, the disdain for closeness and intimacy which shaped his life are alive in the adolescent community today; in some quarters they are idealized and glorified.

Echo Love

My concern in this chapter is not with love itself, but with its adolescent expression. These are not the same, as I hope has been made quite clear by now. Love makes demands on the adolescent character, i.e., self-transcendence, genuine concern for the real needs of the partner, long term commitment, which it rarely can satisfy. During adolescence we see many sides of love, some grand and glorious, some not; among the not is giving one's love to someone who gives nothing in return – Echo love.

Like Echo drawn to Narcissus, girls of today are drawn to beauty and to mystery, and just as Echo could not initiate her own speech, many young girls today cannot initiate their own ideas, or follow their own ambitions; they so lack direction that they willingly, even eagerly, allow another to navigate their course for them. We learn something about this process when we take a look at shy youngsters who are secretive about their yearnings and cravings, indeed all of their feelings. Shy youngsters are awkward in interpersonal settings and often behave inappropriately. They are slow to start conversations, and when they do they speak less than non-shy people; they make less eye contact, show fewer emotions, and smile less. Shy people, like so many adolescents, are uneasy in social situations, they vacillate between fear and interest, avoidance and approach; they are fearful of a social mistake, of ridicule or humiliation. They are not paralyzed, but they are drastically inhibited. *To venture outward they first must be drawn out of themselves, reassured and comforted, put at ease:*

> most shy people strongly desire to get along with others, to have friends and lovers, and to experience intimacy, but they are afraid that they will make a bad impression and experience rejection, humiliation, ostracism, and anxiety. They are painfully aware of how they might be perceived by others, and they constantly fear that others might see them in a bad light. They focus on avoiding anything that might produce rejection or embarrassment. (Baumeister, 1991, p. 53)

These youngsters are not the norm, but neither are they rare. They yearn to be rescued from the prison of their own shyness, but they need to be coddled and flattered before they can risk sharing themselves. Yet when someone takes the time and effort to seek them out, to meet them on their ground, and to allay their anxieties, their allegiance and loyalty are often given freely. For shy youngsters these first moments of glorious sharing may occur with a partner who has cultivated them for private gain. Narcissists "open" their friends in order to exalt themselves, but in the shy one the experience creates a deep gratitude which expresses itself in fidelity, in adulation, and with surprising frequency, in subservience. For many young Echoes this is the stuff of their first adolescent bondings, and it sets the stage for their future love relationships.

Youngsters who do not feel themselves, who have no zest for life, who are morose and depressed, are drawn to the few who can arouse their spirit and excite their passion. The allure is in the sizzle, in the thrill of exploding possibility.[2] But the object of one's devotion may prove unworthy. "Unfortunately, the objects of an adolescent crush are not always protective and caring persons. They may, in fact, have been chosen precisely for the allure of their narcissistic aloofness and grandiosity . . . In the adolescent girl's revering gaze they find a mirror for their narcissistic needs" (Kaplan, 1984, p. 176).

We learn something about Echo love when we consider the low self-esteem for which adolescent girls are rightly known in our culture. It has been something of a mystery for the past decade or so, why girls, upon entry into junior high (grades seven through nine) suddenly begin to exhibit what is generally called "low self-esteem." Considerable debate rages about this loss of self-esteem, including whether it even exists. In regard to the shortage of self-esteem among teen girls, the following are a few observations.

Teenage girls in our culture experience low self-esteem because, as a rule, they don't do anything worthy of esteem in a healthy person. Their day-to-day activities are more child-like than adult-like. Their primary means of escaping their insignificant status are employment, peer popularity, or attachment to a boy. These strategies, as a rule, do very little for genuine self-esteem. Teen employment, except for the poor, is a hoax. The money earned from it, for the most part, is funneled into adventures in esteem purchase. Peer popularity enhances the esteem of early adolescents more than their mature sisters for the simple reason that as values and goals heighten, the essentially utilitarian approval of unenlightened peers means less and less. Sexual attachments to boys, for the most part, do not enhance self-esteem because the boys to which girls attach themselves tend to be older, better practiced, and better skilled at the power politics of the teen community. When the boys are narcissistic in the way described in "the narcissistic style," the age imbalance punishes the girl even more. The Sufi (Muslim mystics famed for their wisdom) claimed that when the pickpocket meets the saint all he sees are pockets, and this is the plight of girls in the open market of adolescent life. In addition to all this, adolescent girls are hustled into the appearance industry and its hall of mirrors sooner, and with greater force, than boys. These considerations, taken in their totality, create a social milieu which conspires against decent self-respect (a better term, in my estimation, than "self-esteem"). While it is obviously true that some girls attain a dramatic upsurge in their self-esteem from employment, from peer popularity, and from boyfriends, these connections often insult their esteem more than they nourish it.

From this vacuous existence the allure of love is irresistible. Love begins with the finding of it, and for this some adolescents are well suited. Even those who cannot speak, like Echo, can find it in those, like Narcissus, who do not speak to them. All of which takes us back to the beginning: adolescent girls in our culture have low self-esteem because their goals, their values, and their behavior are not worthy of esteem. To attain this they must first open their eyes to the emptiness of their day-to-day behavior, choose goals which are inherently worthy and not mere social contrivances, and finally, they must learn to hold boys to a standard of conduct which enhances the dignity of both partners in the relationship. Until these changes are effected, adolescence will contin-ue to be an emotional wasteland for girls, and their dismal self-esteem will continue to accurately reflect the emptiness of their lives.

Bonding Through Giving

> To give love is to get love, and to get love is to be assured of one's lovable-ness . . . (Karl Meninger)

It was Leo Tolstoy who wrote: "We do not love people so much for the good they have done us, as for the good we have done them." This thoughtful aphorism, like all insights which convey wisdom without explaining it, con-tains more than a kernel of truth for adolescents bondings.

We start with the fact that many teens are compassionate and giving by nature. Giving and sharing are to them simply a matter of human policy, a way of greeting life, and of giving themselves over to others. *Giving is as natural to them as receiving is to narcissists.* These are the youth Alfred Adler opti-mistically (but somewhat naively) envisioned all youth to be. Narcissists, as we by now must surely recognize, are the diametric opposite of these gentle souls, since their basic reflexes are not to give, but to take.

Narcissists bond only with those who willingly give, a fact of their nature which, ironically, encourages their giving friends to give even more. Since nar-cissists understand friendship in completely utilitarian terms, they may or may not respect the person who gives; on the other hand, giving, sharing individu-als presume that their gifts are appreciated not merely as gifts, but as an exten-sion of the giver. They assume that it is *they* as well as the gift that is appreci-ated. When their gifts bring pleasure they assume that they are part of the pleasure. This presumption is completely without foundation as far as the nar-cissistically selfish are concerned. To them friends are providers; necessary, but replaceable, providers. Giving youth cannot grasp the idea that they are completely interchangeable with anyone else. Their lack of experience, their egocentrism, and their self-dignity prevent them from understanding how someone could be so completely different from themselves. Their failure to grasp this mystery places them at risk in their dealings with individuals dom-inated by the narcissistic style.

Holding back the desire to give is not an admirable trait, but a complete-ly necessary one when dealing with narcissists. They take more than anyone can possibly give, and they do it smoothly and naturally because they believe that they are entitled, that they are heroically special, that they are more wor-thy than anyone else.

The narcissistically selfish are attracted to the developmentally immature, an attraction which is one of the most significant in the youth culture because it creates unfair and distorted power relationships, especially when mid-ado-lescent (and younger) girls are attracted to late-adolescent boys and young men. The younger partners are drawn to the status, the maturity and the functional wealth of age. This juvenile fascination is not lost on seventeen to twenty-two-year-old males; indeed, in the youth culture, they have perhaps the keenest eye for it.[3]

The equation is simple: the selfish know what they need and they have a plan to get it. In the teen world this places them in a position of considerable advantage because many kids have absolutely no blueprint, no compass. To steer these directionless souls to one's own course is easy, as they have no course of their own, yet they so hunger for a destination they will follow an offered path just to see where it goes.

Of course, other forces are at work in this process. Narcissists presume that because of their specialness, they should associate only with people who are "in a class by themselves"; therefore, the people with whom they associate are granted these qualities (even if only verbally). Because the selfish ones are so heroically special, anyone who flatters them, gives their allegiance to them, automatically becomes greater than the "worthless others" who do not. The fears and insecurities which gnaw at early- and middle-teens are lessened by the Grand One who, through scorn and contempt, reduces everything outside his circle to zero. The selfish friend becomes, in effect, the great leveler of social differences; in a world dominated by status and popularity, this is no small accomplishment, and one which invites and entices, as every Echo willingly confesses.[4]

Final Comments

Our concern here is not with love as much as with one of its tragic imperfections – Echo love.

Echo was a beautiful maiden who "fell in love" with a narcissistic beauty who gave her nothing despite her willingness to give him everything. Ovid, the myth's creator, penned Echo into anorexic nothingness for her reckless squandering of her love and her youth on a vain, self-obsessed young man.

Unless Ovid's myth flowered only from his fertile imagination, we may presume that Echo's naive giving of herself, and Narcissus' selfish disregard of it, has a long history in Western culture. If it doesn't, if it is mere fancy, it certainly is easy enough to find its parallel in today's youth culture.

Narcissists need the allegiance of peers (and lovers) to handle their own insecurities, a need which makes them openly court new clients, and to state openly and boldly: "I want you. I need you. I love you." Such overtures are beautiful music to youth who want to share themselves, to give themselves, and who need nothing more than an earnest invitation. What greater way to know that one is worthy than to hear: "I want you. I need you. I love you."

If it sounds true, if it feels true, then it must be true.

Anecdotes and Supplemental Information

[1]**Adult narcissism**. That adults are also attracted to narcissists is a worthwhile topic, but it is not for this discussion; our concern is with how the attraction of the young to narcissists is influenced by their developmental limitations, their social immaturity, and their limited ability to read the motives of individuals with whom they are connected emotionally.

[2]**The quest for feeling**. Whether feeling is positive and affirmative or negative and depressing is not as significant as feeling itself. In adolescence the quest for feeling is so powerful that *feeling becomes an end in itself*. Hence the attraction to whatever, or whoever, produces feeling.

[3]**Younger female, older male**. The attraction of younger females (approximately from 13-16 years) to older males (approximately 17-20 years) is one of the most self-destructive attractions in the adolescent community. The developmental differences between these age groups is so great as to place the male in a position of power (both intellectually and socially) over the female. The human consequences of this power imbalance are not totally predictable, but they rarely are to the girl's advantage, and they rarely serve her long-term best interests. Consider pregnancy:

> . . . research data indicate that a significant number of adolescent girls are impregnated by males who are at least five years older. Are these pregnancies the result of sexual exploitation or merely of inappropriate dating relationships? (Musick, 1993, p. 86)

[4]**Narcissistic manipulation**. During adolescence the bonds of closeness forged during a two-or-three-month period may take two or three years to untangle. The virtues of decency in ordinary kids are too deep for them to walk away from narcissistic peers who would walk away from them in a minute. Hence, they remain vulnerable to their overtures, to their special requests, to their impassioned pleas for one final, special favor.

[5]**The difference between emotionalism and romanticism**. Some scholars think youth "romantic" because they are so richly attuned to their feelings, and because their behaviour is so greatly influenced by them. However, "emotionally rich" and "romantic" are different things altogether.

Emotionalism has as its ground zero the self, its feelings, and, most importantly, its needs. Romanticism, on the other hand, is an attitude toward life and love which grows from priorities which favour feeling over reason, sentiment over impartiality, subjectivity over objectivity, imagination over reality, intuition over evidence, mysticism over traditional religion, erotic love over security, the natural over the artificial, spontaneity over calculation. Romanticism is grounded in the glory of life; emotionalism in the glory of experience.

A "romantic" embraces the beauty, the mystery, and the sorrow of life guided by an attitude about how life should be lived. One may be both romantic and emotional, indeed, romantics usually are quite emotional; but richness of emotion does not make one a romantic any more than compassion makes one a philanthropist, or anger makes one a warrior. Teens are emotional, but they are not romantic.

Thirteen

Concluding Remarks:

The Mental and Emotional Life Of Teens

Here, in the final chapter, I wish to share with you some of my general conclusions about the forces which shape the thinking, the morals, the behavior, and the misbehavior of teens.

Great as the differences are between the individual and the group, the bias of psychology has always been to learn as much as possible about the individual and then to proceed outward with this knowledge to understand the collective; this has been our approach in this text, and I hope that it has been productive. Certainly no clear line of demarcation has been drawn between the individual teen and the teen culture, but our focus has been on the individual, and the dynamics of individual behavior. Our guiding principle has been that the mental and emotional forces which shape the individual adolescent also shape the entire youth culture.

This book is divided into two broad areas covering the mental and emotional life of teens. The first provides us with a look at the higher levels of adolescent intelligence, and the mechanisms of counter-intelligence which undermine it. The second provides a look at the dynamics of adolescent friendship and love. I have tried to make the case that adolescent intelligence, adolescent selfishness, and adolescent friendship all interact with one another to produce much of what is called "the adolescent experience." When all is said and done, this book is about the highs and lows of adolescent intelligence, and the joys and tribulations of adolescent friendship.

The Mental Life of Teens

In our attempt to understand teen behavior, we are frustrated by the fact that every aspect of their daily life, including their manners, morals and beliefs are governed by a mental apparatus that is seriously flawed. This is not merely to say that adolescent thought is imperfect or imprecise – that would be only to say that it is human. But, the thinking and reasoning processes of adolescence are *predisposed* to make significant errors. This *predisposition* toward mental error is a defining hallmark of the individual adolescent and of adolescent life in general. No real understanding of adolescent life can be achieved without taking into account the mental operations which govern it.

In the first section of this book I tried to explain why adolescents have so much trouble thinking clearly. In the briefest possible summary, the following points and principles informed our look at this topic. First, adolescent thought is egocentric, lacking in perspective, and constrained by limited experience. Second, adolescent thought is vulnerable to fables, such as the "I-will-not-get-pregnant" fable, and the "I-am-invulnerable" fable. Third, adolescent thought periodically becomes awash in emotion, prompting a rise in affective reasoning and a decline in objective reasoning. Fourth, adolescents argue unfairly, and try to incite anger in their opponents, making it difficult for them to debate issues evenly and honestly. Fifth, adolescents harbor a fear of reason and the reasoning process, and this, in turn, encourages cynicism, nihilism, and fatalism in their thinking process. These thought limitations, even one at a time, are troublesome as far as clear thinking is concerned; collectively, they erode decision-making and degrade problem solving.

However, before we become unfairly obsessed with the flaws and limitations of adolescent thought, we ourselves need to step back for a moment to gather perspective, and to make sure that we see these limitations in their proper context. Foremost on our list of considerations, if we are to be fair, is that the adolescent thought process is not universally flawed; its weaknesses are not perpetual, but episodic, expressing themselves in an uneven ebb and flow. Next, alongside these thought limitations rise a host of intellectual strengths and reasoning talents which, when working at full force, produce thought as sophisticated as that of young adults. At its best, adolescent thought is a legitimate and powerful force in the intellectual world; at its worst, it is narcissistic, self-defeating, and as inept and clumsy as its worst stereotypes portray it.

The predicament facing those of us in the business of coaching, teaching, training, and parenting adolescents is this: How can we encourage the adolescent mind to transcend, to triumph over, its own limitations? Equally important: How can we, as outsiders, know when adolescent thinking is guided by strength and when by weakness? These questions are on the mind of parents and teachers and they deserve answers.

We will begin to answer these questions by taking a look at the strengths of adolescent intelligence, for the plain working truth is that most of the problems of youth exist in converse proportion to the proficiency of their thinking, which is to say that as thinking becomes more objective and impartial problems lessen, as it becomes more protectionist, they increase.

The Higher Reaches of Adolescent Intelligence

If one is serious about creating an environment where adolescents behave intelligently, one must know how they reason and how they make sense out of their world. The first step in this process is to learn something about the set of mental operations known as *formal thought*, the name given to the heroic advance in intellectual power which emerges during early adolescence. Aside from puberty, formal thought is the most profound transformation of the adolescent period, and no real understanding of adolescence is possible without taking it into account. Formal thought is the raw material of higher intelligence, of expanded morality, of self-identity, and of self-definition. It fuels the adolescent personality as capital ignites a growing economy.

The higher reaches of adolescent intelligence are determined, in great measure, by five competencies, which, taken in their totality, comprise "formal thought." Here is a brief overview of these mental competencies. (Complete coverage is found in Chapter One).

- **The competency of abstraction.** When development proceeds on schedule, and the environment is not unduly oppressive, adolescents shed the rigid armor of concrete thought for a more flexible, abstract style of thinking. As abstract thought increases, teen thinking shifts in gradual increments away from the here-and-now to the there-and-then, from the practical to the principled, from immediate fact to remote probability. "Adolescents begin to see the particular reality in which they live as one of only several imaginable realities. This leads at least some of them to think about alternative organizations of the world and about deep questions concerning the nature of existence, truth, justice and morality" (Siegler, 1986, p. 41). In other words, adolescent thought matures in its capacity to understand, to engineer, and to honor the abstract.

- **The competency of comprehensiveness.** Compared with children, adolescents think things through in a more thorough and systematic manner; they embrace a larger range of data, and their thought is less susceptible to errors of omission. Which is to say that they take thoroughness and comprehensiveness into the tissues of their living mind.

- **The competency of self-analysis**. Adolescent intelligence shines inward, illuminating inner recesses of the personality heretofore devoid of cerebral light. Children have no such capacity for introspection and self-analysis. Adolescents begin to grasp thought as process; they realize that a particular thought may be rich or poor, weak or strong, developed or undeveloped. They evaluate thought by standards other than the authoritarian or the autocratic. Self-analysis allows thought to recognize and evaluate itself; in this process adolescents not only search for truth, they stamp and approve their particular version of it.

- **The competency of propositional thought.** A proposition is any statement capable of being believed, doubted, denied or argued; propositional thought allows one to investigate reality beyond presently understood boundaries. Basically, propositional thought allows the mind to reason about anything and everything.

Children are not gifted thinkers because they focus mainly on the perceptible elements of a problem, and tend not to speculate about possibilities which do not bear on the matter at hand. They solve problems with few systematic strategies; they rarely have an organized game plan for solving problems. When they solve a problem correctly they often do not know how they solved it, or when faced with a similar problem, they may not be able to beckon the strategies that worked only a few minutes before. Adolescents, on the other hand, can investigate even the most intricate problems matter-of-factly and diligently because of their ability to manipulate propositions.

• **The competency of future analysis.** It is particularly important to understand the significance of future analysis if we are to recognize how the thinking of adolescents soars beyond the thinking of children. Children are not chained to the present, but neither are they free to take flight from it. Formal thinkers, on the other hand, are liberated from the clock, even the calendar; they glide through light years, infinity, timelessness in ways that concrete thinkers cannot even begin to envision. During adolescence immediate time is recognized as a flickering instant of eternal time, and clock time is differentiated from experiential time. The adolescent's transformation to future-oriented thought is profound for many reasons, the most important being that thought and ambition remain primitive until they transcend the immediacy (and the urgency) of present time.[1]

In the end we come to see that formal thought permits the adolescent to venture beyond the real to investigate the ideal, to peer beyond the physical to investigate the hypothetical, to go beyond fragments to investigate wholes, to leap from "what is" to "what if." All in all, these mental skills give the adolescent impressive intellectual credentials, indeed, they are the building blocks for every branch of philosophy and every discipline of science, and they form the intellectual foundation for personal morality and social ideology.[2] These intellectual advances are the infrastructure for the higher reaches of human intelligence. If they were not vulnerable to break down at critical moments, and if they were not undermined by egocentrism, narcissism, and emotionality, adolescence would be a far easier time of life. But they are, and it isn't.

Obstacles to Reaching Higher Levels of Intelligence

I think there is only one quality worse than hardness of heart and that is softness of head. (Theodore Roosevelt)

Despite its great forward surge, everyone is fully aware that adolescent thinking is not always clear nor coherent. Upon close inspection we find that murky thinking, "softness of head," usually occurs under the following conditions:

• when the adolescent abandons the "checks and balances," and other methods of verification and validation inherent to formal thought;

• when the adolescent employs affective reason more than objective reason;

• when the adolescent understands an issue in terms of how it effects "me" rather than in terms of the issue itself;

• when thought is blocked by protectionism; and,

• when the adolescent uses fables and fictions to divine unexplained mysteries.

An important lesson we have learned from the study of adolescent psychology over the past five decades is that while the deficiencies of adolescent thinking are correctable, few of them are self-correcting. The *potential* for clear thinking is natural, but before this potential can be actualized, it requires good mentoring, and lots of it. The ideal mentor is an adult who can think clearly and who has the best interests of the young person at heart – a parent, a teacher, a coach, a minister, a family friend. Bottom line: higher intelligence, like higher athleticism, must be trained and coached to reach its potential. To expect teens to become proficient thinkers and effective decision-makers on their own is not only unjustified by the available scientific evidence, theoretically, it is preposterous. Naturally this does not please the utopians who believe that, given a safe and protected environment, adolescents will naturally acquire coherence of thought and sanity of decision-making merely from the texture of life. But on this count, the utopians are on the wrong side of the aisle.

•   •   •

An irony of teen life in North American culture is that, generally speaking, faulty thinking carries no significant penalty, and most of the time when teens act impulsively, without thinking, without taking consequences into account, there is no real price to pay for this brashness. However, in selected instances, such mindless impulsivity produces the most serious consequences of the entire life cycle. Let me explain. Nothing carries the lifetime consequences of having a baby, of dropping out of school, of drug addiction, of an automobile or motorcycle accident. This is a way of saying that a string of faulty decisions can be far more disastrous to an adolescent's life than anything positive which could possibly occur because of a string of intelligent decisions. During adolescence bad decisions can produce immediate, destructive consequences; good decisions, on the other hand, produce gradual incre- ments of benefit, but nothing profoundly and immediately positive. Hence, many adolescent-watchers, myself included, believe that the key to teen sur- vival is the avoidance of poor decisions and the negative consequences that come with them. For every youth arrived at age twenty, this involves a con- siderable degree of good fortune, a healthy dose of adult supervision, and a giant portion of clear thinking and effective decision making. The third part, clear thinking and effective decision making, is primary to our discussion, and we have gone to great lengths to describe some of the mental mechanisms which interfere with clear thinking and good decision making, causing ado- lescents to make impulsive and ill-reasoned decisions which place them at-risk for suffering, disease, or death.

Cultivated intelligence is not widespread in the teen community, even though adolescents are blessed with a tremendous potential for it. Like most potential, the intellectual potential of youth must be nurtured and coddled, gleaned and groomed before it can reach its full glory. On its own, in the absence of schooling, training, and mentoring, adolescent intelligence (espe- cially during the early- and middle-years) is immature, shaky, prone to error, and mesmerized by fable, fiction, and fantasy. Adolescent intelligence, gener- ally speaking, is a primitive intelligence constrained by its fear of reason, and narrowed by its narcissism. All of this discussion is necessary to appreciate the anti-rational tendencies which storm through the adolescent intellect. One nourishes, encourages, and glorifies them at a certain peril to that to which they stand in opposition.

The Emotional Life of Teens

Throughout this book I have tried to make the case that the psychology of narcissism overlaps in meaningful ways with the psychology of adolescence, and that when we investigate one we learn about the other. Narcissists are not always adolescents, but adolescents are always narcissistic – at least to some degree. By learning about the narcissism inherent to the adolescent personali- ty, we have gained insight into the adolescent's thinking habits, friendship pat- terns, and intimacy connections.

The study of narcissism has led to the discovery of two basic principles of human behavior, both of which hold significant implications for the psychol- ogy of youth. First, self-obsession creates neither self-love nor self-apprecia- tion. Second, self-obsession and altruism exist in converse proportion to one another – as one goes up the other goes down. These principles deserve thoughtful consideration by any person, group or organization desirous of cre- ating a positive path for teen development to follow. They also serve as a good starting point for an analysis of the youth culture, which, when all is said and done, is little more than the commercial mining of the narcissistic cravings and emotional insecurities of youth.

The Role of Selfishness in the Mental and Emotional Life of Teens

Art thou a silkworm? Dost thou spin thy own shroud out of thyself?
(Hermann Melville)

We understand youth more honestly when we accept that selfishness is one of the defining attributes of their emotional ecology. To help us in this understanding, I have broken it into three categories, (1) developmental self-ishness, (2) pathological selfishness, and (3) the narcissistic style.

Developmental self-ish-ness, is a healthy and necessary component of human development. When we think of it our thoughts are directed to the natural demands of a developing self, to wholesome egoism, to honest self-pride. The term, for me, carries no negative connotations. Developmental self-ish-ness is the trademark of all healthy kids; without it they have no real sense of themselves as important beings. Developmental self-ish-ness displays a healthy narcissism and a legitimate pride. Narcissistic selfishness is another matter altogether.

Narcissistic selfishness is a radical and profound selfishness. When we think of it we think of self-infatuation so extreme that the interests of others are completely ignored. The narcissistically selfish person is always fearful of not getting enough, of being deprived, and is filled with a burning envy of anyone who has more. The narcissistically selfish are unwilling to give but anxious to take. They lack any genuine interest in the welfare of others, and they hold only instrumental respect for human dignity. Narcissistic selfishness, because it is totally self-grounded, is corrosive to morality, to objective intelligence, and to friendship.

At the risk of being repetitious, I want to once again remind the reader that individuals imbued with narcissistic selfishness cannot handle the give and take of normal human relationships. Their first question at every junction is the same: "Is this for me or against me?" They are saddled with unworkable presumptions about human relationships which, with the passage of time, harden into the belief that others must always accommodate to "my" needs, that "my" relevance does not need to be earned or proved, and that from "my" special-ness flows a river of entitlements.

Between the natural developmental self-ish-ness of youth and pathological selfishness lives a unique selfishness I call "the narcissistic style." The *narcissistic style* is not natural in the same way as developmental self-ish-ness, neither is it pathological in the same way as narcissistic selfishness; rather, it is an exaggeration of the former and a lessened version of the latter.

We have given the narcissistic style close examination because of the profound implications it holds for the development of our adolescent children, and because our society seems intent on cultivating it, on pushing kids away from their natural developmental selfishness into the hollow, hostile self-absorption which typifies the youth culture, and which undermines the adolescent's capacity for genuine intimacy and love.

What do we mean when we say that adolescents live by the narcissistic style? What are we saying about their character, manners, morals, intelligence? Typically, five traits define the narcissistic style.

• The narcissistic style hinges on the presumption that "I" am entitled to special treatment, and, that it is the responsibility of others to provide it. This attitude causes youth to see others as providers, and places them in a hostile relationship with everyone who doesn't provide. A distorted view of the balance between what one is owed and what one owes is the starting point of the narcissistic style – *the narcissistic style is characterized by excessive entitlement demands.*[3]

• Individuals with a narcissistic style have little compassion for others. Their view of the world, their likes and dislikes, indeed, their entire consciousness is monopolized by their own thoughts, their own pain, and their own pleasure. Hence, they are impervious to the feelings and needs of others - *the narcissistic style is characterized by insensitivity to the feelings of others.*

• In the narcissistic style one accepts love without giving much of it in return. Narcissistic youth do not oppose love in that they willingly receive it – their failure is in their inability to give it. They are lovers in part but not in whole; a fact of their nature which is remarkably immune to detection by other teens - *the narcissistic style is characterized by the reduced capacity to give love.*

It is generally recognized that morality involves several preconditions including fear of punishment, the desire to belong and fit into a group, an autonomous conscience, and belief in a higher authority. The morality of adolescents driven by the narcissistic style is different. How? Narcissistic morality serves the self. To think of narcissists as completely without morality is too severe; that, after all, would make them psychopaths - but it is fair to report that they occupy only a limited number of floors in the tower of morality. Narcissism is antithetical to morality because it places self above everything else.

• Many youngsters have what, on first glance, looks like genuine morality because they describe everyday events in the language of good/bad, right/wrong, worthy/unworthy. Every action *which affects them* is judged morally. This, of course, is not to say that they are moral persons, if by this we mean that they live by a code of honor, or believe in a higher authority. When we look closely at these youth what we really see is *moralism* rather than morals, *moralizing* rather than morality. Narcissistic morality is little more than a pretense by which to proclaim oneself superior, or to elevate oneself at the expense of another; it is, at heart, not about right or wrong, but about self-protection – *the narcissistic style is characterized by a narrow range of moral concerns.*[4]

• The narcissistic style, by its very nature, is contrary to an informed and friendly intelligence because it perceives reality through the lens of self-enhancement. Narcissists are learning disabled in that they blur objective reality with their own private collection of egocentric prejudices and protective presumptions. They are incapable of intellectual balance or moral fairness – *the narcissistic style is characterized by a lessened capacity for objective thought.*

The narcissistic style is encouraged by the images of advertising and by the cravings nurtured by consumerism, pop culture, and the psychology of immediacy, but it is not *caused* by any of them. These conditions hurry the narcissistic impulse, but they do not create it. Adolescents gravitate to narcissistic images because their egocentrism, their developmental selfishness, and their narcissism impel them in this direction. Adolescents are predisposed to embrace narcissistic gratifiers, and to encourage this predisposition is as easy as teaching a toddler to be right-handed. The narcissistic impulse comes from the inner self, but it is encouraged by the offerings of the outer world. The youth culture, when we see it for what it is, is little more than a creation by the dominant culture to profit financially from the narcissism and the insecurity of youth.

The main current of thought on this topic, to which all others are mere tributaries, is this: the emotional health of adolescents cannot be separated from the nature and degree, of their selfishness.

Psychological Health and Selfishness. The following chart helps us to envision the relationship between selfishness and psychological health. The top line represents a continuum of health ranging from normal psychological functioning through psychiatric disorder, i.e., from healthy to unhealthy. The bottom line represents the continuum of selfishness, ranging from normal developmental selfishness through pathological selfishness, i.e., from healthy to unhealthy. The categories on each continuum match those directly above (or below).

Psychological Health

Normal psychological functioning.........Borderline........Psychiatric disorder

Selfishness

Developmental Selfishness.....The Narcissistic Style.....Pathological Selfishness

---

The Search for Meaning and Importance

Part of the difficulty with being an adolescent in our society is that adults themselves do not understand the differences between self-importance and self-aggrandizement. They think that anything that makes adolescents feel good about themselves is a step in the right direction, and this is not right. We adults are so concerned that teens feel important that we lose sight of *what they feel important about.* Self-importance can never be separate from *what one does.* Quite frankly, social workers, high school teachers and parents are broken from dealing with youngsters whose sense of self-importance has been warped by consumerism, corrupted by violence, and degraded by pregnancy fables. Youth want to feel important but they don't know the first thing about important behavior – except that deemed important in their isolated peer group, or valorized in popular culture. In this area of their life – the quest for legitimate importance – adolescents require considerable guidance, supervision, and direction. To think they will find it on their own is as naïve as to think they will avoid pregnancy, death by vehicle, or drug contamination on their own. Many do, of course. But those who don't number in the millions in North American culture.

Genuine self-importance flows from the worthwhile actions one actually accomplishes; unfortunately, in the adolescent community little opportunity arises to build useful products or to assert oneself affirmatively. As a society we simply do not provide youth with opportunities to act adult in important and constructive ways. Without meaningful work and constructive participation, young people try to wrangle meaning from consumer goods, from peer approval, from adventures in intimacy. Who could have summarized it better than Albert Einstein? "Only a life lived for others is a life worthwhile." The predicament of many adolescents is that they have not received adequate training from their parents as to what is, and what is not, "a life worthwhile." Conformity without conviction inevitably leads to boredom, and the need to escape the boredom inherent to purposeless life is the real problem for contemporary youth.

The conclusion to emerge from all this is that youth who do not make real contributions to their family or their society, experience an emptiness they try to fill through narcissistic inflation. This attempt is doomed since the surface sensations and visual images of narcissistic inflation simply cannot nourish the moral, spiritual, and love needs of the adolescent personality.

We may sum up with two simple principles of adolescent life:

1. As important behavior decreases, self-fixation increases.

2. As important behavior increases, self-fixation decreases.

The obsession with narcissistic stimulation so evident in the youth culture, is, in part, a response to the fact that adolescent life in our culture lacks meaningful contribution, worthwhile work, genuine family and community significance. The pathos of youth springs not so much from a deficiency within their nature as an emptiness within their culture.

Togetherness, Friendship and Love

The desire to fuse with another self and to share in the pleasure of this union is an honorable and decent part of human nature. In real life, the conjoinment is not always ideal – especially during adolescence when the demands of friendship often exceed the young person's mental and emotional resources. Adolescent friendship is not a final destination in human bonding. It is an internship for learning some of the necessary skills required to master the more advanced, more intricate, and more demanding relationships of adulthood.

Younger adolescents express their need for companionship and togetherness in ways profoundly different from older adolescents. Early adolescents are too engrossed in the responsibility of their own growth and development to be effective in their knowledge of others. They are handicapped in the task of self-knowledge because their self, like their body, grows and changes so rapidly that the constancy required for convincing knowledge is simply not available to them. As knowledge about the feelings of others matures during the course of childhood, so knowledge about intimacy matures during the course of adolescence. (See [4] at the end of Chapter Ten for a more thorough overview of the differences among early-, middle-, and late-adolescents.)

Our understanding of adolescent friendship is bolstered when we take into account the following:

• All youngsters need friendship, intimacy, and love for their proper development, but satisfying these needs is complicated by the adolescent's egocentric narrowness.

• Adolescent friendship often requires each partner to give approval in exchange for it being returned. Convincing a friend that defects are really virtues, in exchange for the friend doing the same, is a duty for many teens.

• Adolescents are inherently attracted to companions who respect them, who praise them, and who flatter them, but it often takes a considerable period of time for the adolescent to learn who is praising, who is flattering, and who is respecting. During this period of time the adolescent is prone to poor friendship selection, and if the friendship turns romantic, poor intimacy decisions.

• The most exploitive relationships in the adolescent community exist between late-adolescent boys and early-adolescent girls. These relationships may be accepted among the teens involved, but almost always their bond is melded by the younger girl's illusion that the boy is as grand and glorious as she imagines him to be. Sometimes he is, but usually he isn't, and the younger girl typically pays the greater price.

• The mental errors which frequent the adolescent thought process occur with even greater persistence when friendship or intimacy are the object of thought. As a result, teen friendships are rarely seen for what they are. So long as self-knowledge is under-developed, so also is knowledge of friendship.

• Teens characterized by the normal self-centredness we call "developmental selfishness," are not nearly as self-promoting and boorishly demanding as youth impelled by "the narcissistic style." Unfortunately, individuals with the narcissistic style consistently solicit their partners from the ranks of the developmentally selfish, which leads to friendships grounded in imbalance and unfairness.

These intricate subplots – the conflict between togetherness and selfishness, the need to give approval in order to receive it, the politics of synchronized deception, the exploitation of the younger by the older – are major players in the rise and fall of teen friendship. Without giving them fair analysis, the politics of youth defy comprehension.[5]

Intimacy does not blossom until *both* partners have attained a certain maturity of identity. This claim was first defended in developmental psychology by Erik Erikson, but it is a claim which fits well with our current understanding of the mental and emotional life of teens. It poses real problems for teens for reasons already discussed, notably that they often bond with narcissistic partners, or with partners too immature to possess a solid, unified identity. Mature intimacy requires mutuality, reciprocity, and an honest concern for the real needs of the partner. H. S. Sullivan put it this way, "intimacy requires a clearly formulated adjustment of one's behavior to the *expressed needs of the other person* in the pursuit of increasingly identical, that is *more and more nearly mutual satisfactions."*

Adolescents believe Sullivan's point in theory more than they act on it in practice. Teens with the weakest identity are often the ones who most desperately crave intimacy. They believe emotional intimacy and sexual intimacy are one and the same, and that sexual intercourse is love's calling card. For millions of North American youth, this is the most profound mental error of their lives.

Friendship, intimacy, and love are painfully complicated by the uneven levels of mental and emotional maturity in teen society. Some teens have made great strides in their identity quest, hold a solid sense of themselves, and speak honestly to the question "Who am I?" They have a good idea where they are going and hold examined thoughts about how to get there. Others, quite literally, haven't got a clue. They have nothing that resembles a solid sense of themselves, their identity has made few real strides, and the primary question "Who am I?" is met with a blank tilt of the chin. They have no culture beyond pop culture, marginal impulse control, and fear everything that threatens their narrowness. Even their peers think of them as stunted and impervious to the meaningful.[6] These youth, different as they are, do not live in mutually exclusive worlds, quite the contrary, they share friendships and they participate in each other's lives, some even fall in love with each other; in this mix the primitive ones are pulled upward and the mature ones tugged downward in a youthful dance of convergence and complementarity.

In the midst of all these far-reaching ideas, we remain bound to the basic, unalterable fact of adolescence: it is a time of life for making progress toward a destination greater than adolescence itself. Adolescents are not final products, they are works in progress. The next stop in their developmental progression is early-adulthood, and the quality of intelligence, the breadth of morality, and the decency of friendship which they exhibit at this critical life intersection is determined, in very great measure, by how meaningfully their intelligence, their morality, and their friendships were nurtured during adolescence.

Anecdotes and Supplemental Information

[1] **Future Pull – the role of the future in facing the present.** Youth do not, and cannot, live entirely in the present. They visualize and anticipate their future, assessing in their own minds what it holds for them. Future assessment is an intrinsic and inevitable feature of adolescent intelligence.

The ability to tolerate pain, cope with stress, and endure anxiety is related to one's perception of where one is going. The more optimistically and openly one faces the future, the greater the ability to cope with adversity in the present; contrariwise, the more grimly one faces the future, the more overpowering is present pain. For youth, the formula is elementary: when the future is filled with promise and high expectation, the turmoil and anxiety of everyday living is placed in perspective; when the future is perceived as holding little promise for growth or self-assertion, the anxiety of present time becomes the central fact of life – nothing cushions its intensity and no feeling of future liberation relieves its distress.

Youth are pulled toward the future by their *biology*. They are growing, unfolding, and expanding; therefore, to know ones self as an adolescent is to know that the future is essential for completion of the bodily self. Youth are biologically incomplete and they know it; the future holds their body.

Youth are pulled toward the future by their *psychology*. The need for intimacy increases throughout the course of adolescence. "I-ness" is gradually being replaced with "we-ness," and until this metamorphosis occurs, the self is incomplete. Youth anticipate the future because without it they are not yet themselves.

Youth are pulled toward the future by their *morality*. Shedding the moral dogmatism of childhood, teens search for viable explanations and viewpoints; uncertain as to what is right or wrong, they formulate moral codes which balance impulse with outcome, pleasure with principle.

Future time is an essential parcel in the adolescent package; optimal growth does not take place when the future is feared or deemed unworthy. Youth need to believe that the future will not deny them acceptance, esteem, love, and meaningful work. When the future is perceived as holding chains, but not keys, adolescent growth grinds to a halt. The present rules because it has been stripped of the only thing that gives it meaning – the future.

[2]**How moral outlook changes during the course of adolescence.** During adolescence five important changes take place in moral outlook which, in large measure, account for the differences between child and adolescent morality. In the absence of these developmental progressions, late adolescents are no more advanced morally than early adolescents. These changes include: (a) moral outlook becomes progressively more abstract and less concrete; (b) moral outlook becomes more concerned with right, less concerned with wrong; justice emerges as the prevailing moral concept; (c) moral outlook becomes increasingly cognitive - the adolescent analyses moral codes more analytically and more comprehensively than during childhood; (d) moral outlook increasingly incorporates the perspectives of others, thus becoming less egocentric; (e) moral outlook becomes emotionally expensive – childhood morality is fairly emotion free as children do not wrestle with moral dilemmas, nor do they see easily alternatives to their own moral viewpoints, consequently, during childhood, morality is "pain free".

[3]**Rights, benefits and the attitude of entitlement.** Teens easily embrace the idea that they are *entitled* to extra benefits and special rights. They do not have to be taught this attitude – they are developmentally predisposed to it by their egocentrism, their lack of perspective-taking, their need to affirm themselves, and their tendency, retained from childhood, to perceive adults only as providers. These predispositions can be lessened by effective teaching, by seeing from another's perspective, by having a safe and secure environment, by working on worthwhile projects, and by participating meaningfully in the lives of others.

[4]**The adolescent's concern with justice.** The narcissistic style is especially burdensome to moral development because it contradicts many of the advances typically made during adolescence. For example, the adolescent's concern with justice. If fairness is the dominant moral abstraction of childhood, justice is the dominant moral abstraction of adolescence. Intellectual expansiveness leads most youth to realize that justice is not merely self-protection, but a principle applied to all. From this intellectual awakening, social justice emerges as a dominant theme of adolescent morality – especially during the middle and late-adolescent years.

A trend worth nothing is the adolescent's reduced preoccupation with wrong and increased concern with right. Teens become more impressed with the right doings of others (as judged by their own understanding of what is right) and less overwhelmed by wrongdoings. Their growing awareness of the relativity of moral values provides them with a more tolerant attitude toward the vices of others. They are impressed with good behavior when they see it. They increasingly see the goodness of the person without accepting the person's beliefs, and vice-versa. Such moral complexity is beyond the child's grasp.

[5]**To the subplots of adolescent friendship we could easily add the fear of humiliation.** Teens fear humiliation in every way, shape, or form; a fear which leads to their refusal to participate in relationships where humiliation might possibly occur. They seem to operate on the belief that any less-than-perfect performance will shower shame or ridicule upon them. Self-image is part of the problem. "Obsession with an image of yourself can make you so sensitive to criticism that ordinary give and take is humiliating and you avoid people. . . . Teenagers trapped with this defense certainly cannot be loose and spontaneous. . . . An over concern with your image exacerbates feelings of shame. Some cannot even ask a question, for not to know is to admit being less than perfect. Others cannot acquire skills. To practice a sport means living through a period of looking bad" (Polansky, 1991, p. 74).

Louise Kaplan adds this: "Another reason for the increased self-centredness of an adolescent is her susceptibility to humiliation. This brazen, defiant creature is also something tender, raw, thin-skinned, poignantly vulnerable. Her entire sense of personal worth can be shattered by a frown. An innocuous clarification of facts can be heard as a monumental criticism" (1984, p. 189).[6]

In his insightful paper "Normal and pathological narcissism in adolescence," (1994) Efrain Bleiberg claimed: "Perhaps like no other phase of life, the passage through adolescence bears the hallmarks of narcissistic vulnerability: a proneness to embarrassment and shame, acute self-consciousness and shyness, and painful questions about self-esteem and self-worth." He could easily have added another: the fear of humiliation.

[6]**The imperviousness of youth is of two distinct types.** Blank imperviousness is a form of mental withdrawal into one's own feelings and moods; a way of turning off the outside world by disengaging one's mind, leaving it blank. A mental rest stop on the information highway with a touch of half-awake daydreaming. Blank imperviousness is a harmless, perhaps even necessary, removal of oneself from the immediate sensory world. It is a common mental state for children, adolescents and adults. Narcissistic imperviousness is tuning the world out in order to become more attuned to one's inner emotional sensations. It is not "blank" at all, rather, it is a state of self-arousal and self-absorption so fixed that it cancels everything which does not feed it. It exhibits a deep, determined, indifference to life outside its boundaries. Narcissistic imperviousness is not boredom, nor is it mere passive indifference; it is an active mental investment which requires energy and effort to be sustained. It is much more than mere blank imperviousness, and to envision it this way is to miss its essential character – emotive self-immersion.

Narcissistic imperviousness is the turning away from, the indifference to, the neutralization of, and the dismissal of anything which gets in the way of one's own self-absorption. It is a form of withdrawal the adolescent calls upon when reality is painful, ego-diminishing, or when it merely opposes one's self. Narcissistic imperviousness scorns everything which stands in the way of the self bathing in its own sensations.

Bibliography

Adler, A. (1939). *Social interest.* New York, NY: Putnam.

Alford, F.C. (1988). *Narcissism.* New Haven, CT: Yale University Press.

American Psychiatric Association. (1994). *Diagnostic and statistical manual of mental disorders (4th ed.). DSM-IV.* Washington, DC: American Psychiatric Association.

Anderson, J. (1993). *A study of "out-of-the mainstream" youth in Halifax, Nova Scotia.* Halifax, NS: Health and Welfare Canada.

Arnett, J. (1992). Reckless behavior in adolescence. *Developmental Review, 12.*

Atwater, E. (1998). *Adolescence.* NJ: Prentice Hall.

Ayers, L.K. (1994). *Teenage girls.* New York, NY: Crossroad Publishing.

Barrett, H. (1991). *Rhetoric and civility.* Albany, NY: State University Press of New York.

Baumeister, R.F. (1991). *Escaping the self.* New York, NY: Basic Books.

Bleiberg, E. (1994). Normal and pathological narcissism in adolescence. *American Journal of Psychotherapy, Vol. 48, No, 1,* Winter 1994.

Brown, B.B., Mory, M.S. & Kinney, D. (1994). Casting adolescent crowds in a relational context: Caricature, channel, and context, in *Personal relationships during adolescence,* Montmeyer, R., ed. Thousand Oaks, CA: Sage.

Brown, R., Keating, S., & O'Connor, J. (1998). Sexual abuse in childhood and subsequent illicit drug abuse in adolescence and early adulthood. *Irish Journal of Psychiatric Medicine, 15(4),* 123-126.

Chomsky, N. (1989). *Necessary illusions.* Boston, MA: South End Press.

Collins, W.A. & Repinski, D.J. (1994). Relationships during adolescence: Continuity and change in interpersonal behavior, in *Personal relationships during adolescence,* Montmeyer, R., ed. Thousand Oaks, CA: Sage.

Cooper, A.M. (1986). Narcissism, in *Essential papers on narcissism,* Morrison, A.P., ed. New York, NY: New York University Press.

Denby, D. (1996). *The New Yorker.* July 15.

Doig, C. & Burgess, E. (2000). Withholding life-sustaining treatment: Are adolescents competent to make these decisions? *Canadian Medical Association Journal, 162(11): 1585-8,* May 2000.

Donaldson, M. (1978). *Children's minds.* Glasgow, Scotland: Fontana.

Driscoll, M.P. (1994). *Psychology of learning.* Boston, MA: Allyn & Bacon.

DuRant, R.H. (1999). Weapon carrying on school property among middle school students. *Archives of Pediatric and Adolescent Medicine, 153,* 21-26.

Dusek, J.B. (1991). *Adolescent development and behavior.* Englewood Cliffs, NJ: Prentice Hall.

Egan, K. (1990). *Romantic understanding.* New York, NY: Routledge.

Elkind, D. (1967). Egocentrism in adolescence. *Child Development, 38,* 1025-1034.

Elkind, D. (1985). Egocentrism redux. *Developmental Review, 5,* 218-226.

Elkind, D. (1987). The child yesterday, today and tomorrow. *Young Children, 42(4),* 6-11.

Erikson, E.H. (1946). Ego development and historical change, in *The psychoanalytic study of the child,* Vol. II. Eissler, R., ed. New York, NY: International Universities Press.

Erikson, E.H. (1956). The problem of ego identity. *Journal of American Psychiatric Association, 4,* 56-121.

Erikson, E.H. (1960). Youth and the life cycle. *Children, 7,* March/April, 43-49.

Erikson, E.H. (1968). *Identity, youth and crisis.* New York, NY: W.W. Norton & Co.

Etzioni, A. (1993). *The spirit of community.* New York, NY: Crown Publishers.

Farris, P.J. (1996). *Teaching, bearing the torch.* Dubuque, IA. Times Mirror Higher Education Group.

Feldman, R.S. & Custrini, R.J. (1988). Learning to lie and self-deceive: Children's nonverbal communication of deception, in *Self-deception: An adaptive mechanism?* Lockard, J.S. & Paulhus, D.L., eds. Englewood Cliffs, NJ: Prentice-Hall.

Fine, R. (1986). *Narcissism, the self and society.* New York, NY: Columbia University Press.

Flavell, J.H. (1963). *The developmental psychology of Jean Piaget.* New York, NY: Van Nostrand.

French. S.A. (1997). Ethnic differences in psychosocial correlates of dieting, purging, and binge eating in a population-based sample of adolescent females. *The International Journal of Eating Disorders, 22(3),* 315-322,

Freud, A. (1966). The ego and the mechanisms of defense, in *The writings of Anna Freud. Vol. 2.* New York, NY: International Universities Press.

Freud, S. (1914). On narcissism. in *On metapsychology.* Harmondsworth, XXX: Penguin, (1984).

Freud, S. (1932). *The ego and the id.* Vol. 19 of *The standard edition.* London, UK: Hogarth.

Friedenberg, E. (1959). *The vanishing adolescent.* New York, NY: Dell.

Fromm, E. (1964). *The heart of man.* New York: Harper & Row.

Fromm, E. (1957). *The art of loving.* New York: Harper & Row.

Fromm, E. (1973). The anatomy of human destructiveness. New York, NY: Holt, Rinehart & Winston.

Frosh, S. (1991). *Identity crisis: Modernity, psychoanalysis and the self.* London: Routledge.

Furnham, A. & Stacey, B. (1991). *Young people's understanding of society.* London, UK: Routledge.

Furman, W. & Werner, E.A. (1994). Romantic views: Toward a theory of adolescent romantic relationships, in *Personal relationships during adolescence,* Montmeyer, R., ed. Thousand Oaks, CA: Sage.

Galambos, N.L., & Tilton-Weaver, L.C. (1998). Multiple-risk behaviour in adolescents and young adults. *Health Reports, (10(2),* 9-20.

Gardner, W. (1993). A life-span rational-choice theory of risk taking, in *Adolescent risk taking,* Bell, N.J., ed. Newbury Park, CA: Sage.

Garrod, A., Smulyan, L., Powers, S. I. & Kilkenny, R. (1992). *Adolescent portraits: Identity relationships, and challenges.* Boston, MA: Allyn and Bacon.

Goldberg, C. (1980). *In defense of narcissism.* New York, NY: Gardner Press.

Goleman, D. (1985). *Vital lies, simple truths.* New York, NY: Simon & Schuster.

Grice, H.P. (1975). Logic and conversation, in *Syntax and semantics: Vol. 3.* Speech acts, Cole, P. & Morgan, J.L., eds. New York, NY: Academic Press.

Grovetant, H.D. (1993). *The integrative nature of identity, in Discussions on ego identity,* Kroger, J., ed. Hillsdale, NJ: Lawrence Erlbaum.

Hamburg, D. A. (1992). *Today's children: Creating a future for a generation in crisis.* New York, NY: Times Books.

Health Canada (1995). *Canadians' Alcohol and Other Drug Use: Increasing Our Understanding* (D. Hewitt, G. Vinje & P. MacNeil, Eds). Ottawa.

Henshaw, S.K. (1997). Teenage Abortion and Pregnancy Statistics by State. *Family Planning Perspectives, 29,* 115-122.

Holmes, J. & Silverman, E.L. (1992). *We're here, listen to us.* Ottawa: Canadian Advisory Council on the Status of Women.

Horney, K. (1937). *The neurotic personality of our time.* New York, NY: W.W. Norton.

Inhelder, B. & Piaget, J. (1958). *The growth of logical thinking.* New York, NY: Basic Books.

Irwin, C.E. (1993). Adolescence and risk taking: How are they related?, in Bell, N.J., *Adolescent risk taking,* Newbury Park, CA: Sage.

Jacoby, M. (1990). *Individuation and narcissism.* New York, NY: Routledge.

Kaplan, L. (1984). *Adolescence: The farewell to childhood.* New York, NY: Touchstone Books.

Kiell, N. (1964). *The universal experience of adolescence.* London, UK: University of London Press.

Kohn, A. (1990). *The Brighter Side of Human Nature.* New York, NY. Basic Books.

kohut, H. (1977). The restoration of self. New York, NY: International University Press.

Lasch, C. (1978). *The culture of narcissism.* New York, NY: W.W. Norton.

Lasch, C. (1984). *The minimal self.* New York, NY: W.W. Norton.

Lees, S. (1986). *Losing out: Sexuality and adolescent girls.* London, UK: Hutchinson.

Lewis, M. (1995). Embarrassment: the emotion of self-exposure and evaluation, in *Self-conscious emotions,* by J.P. Tangney & K. W. Fischer. New York, NY: The Guilford Press.

Lindsay, C. (1994). *Youth in Canada* (2nd ed.). Ottawa, ON: Statistics Canada, Housing, Family and Social Statistics Division.

Lyons, N. (1990). Dilemmas of knowing, CA. *Harvard Educational Review 60* (2): 159-180.

Martin, M.W. (1996). *Love's virtues.* Lawrence, KS: University Press of Kansas.

McAdams, D.P. (1990). *The person.* San Diego: Harcourt Brace Jovanovich.

McGuire, P. (1983). *It won't happen to me: Teenagers talk about pregnancy.* New York, NY: Delacorte.

McWilliams, N. (1994). *Psychoanalytic diagnosis.* New York, NY: Guilford Press.

Millon, T. (1981). Narcissistic personality: The egotistic pattern, in *Disorders of personality DSM-III: Axis II.* New York, NY: John Wiley & Sons.

Mitchell, J.J. (1980). *Child development.* Toronto, ON: Holt, Rinehart & Winston.

Mitchell, J.J. (1985). *The nature of adolescence.* Calgary, AB: Detselig Enterprises.

Mitchell, J.J. (1989). *Human growth and development: The childhood years.* Calgary, AB: Detselig Enterprises.

Monte, C.F. (1991). *Beneath the mask.* Fort Worth, TX: Holt, Rinehart & Winston.

Montmeyer, R. (1994). *Personal relationships during adolescence.* Thousand Oaks, CA: Sage.

Moore, S. & Rosenthal, D. (1993). *Sexuality in adolescence.* London, UK: Routledge.

Moore, T. (1992). *Care of the soul.* New York, NY. Harper Collins.

Moreno, A.B. (1995). Eating Behavior in Junior High School Females. *Adolescence, 30,* 171-174

Muller, H.J. (1960). *Issues of freedom.* New York, NY: Harper & Row.

Munro, B. & Doherty-Poirier, M. (2000). Health Risk Behavior and Identity Formation During Adolescence. Unpublished Concept Paper.

Musick, J.S. (1993). *Young, poor, and pregnant: The psychology of teenage motherhood.* New Haven, CT: Yale University Press.

Muuss, R.E., ed. (1990). *Adolescent behavior and society,* 4th ed. New York, NY: McGraw Hill, Inc.

Nickerson, R.S. (1991). *Some observations on the teaching of thinking, in Enhancing learning and thinking,* Mulcahy, R., ed. New York, NY: Praeger.

Nussbaum, M. (1990). *Love's knowledge: Essays on philosophy and literature.* Oxford, UK: Oxford University Press.

Olgivy, J. (1995). *Living without a goal.* New York, NY. Doubleday.

Pagliaro, A.M. & Pagliaro, L.A. (1993). Knowledge, behaviors, and risk perceptions of intravenous drug users in relation to HIV infection and AIDS. *Advances in Medical Psychotherapy, 6,* 1-28.

Paulson, S.E., and Sputa, C.L. (1996). Patterns of Parenting During Adolescence. *Adolescence, 31,* 369-381.

Perry, C. N. and McIntire, W. G. (1995). Modes of Moral Judgment among Early Adolescents. *Adolescence, 30,* 707-715.

Peterson, K. L. (1991). Imaginary Audience Behavior in Older Adolescent Females. *Adolescence, 26,* 195-200.

Phoenix, A. (1991). *Young mothers.* Cambridge, UK: Polity Press.

Piaget, J. (1928). *Judgment and reasoning in the child.* New York, NY. Harcourt Brace Jovanovich.

Piaget, J. (1967). The mental development of the child, in *Six psychological studies* by Piaget, Elkind, D., ed. New York, NY: Random House.

Piaget, J. & Inhelder, B. (1958). *The growth of logical thinking.* New York, NY: Basic Books.

Piatelli-Palmarini, M. (1994). *Inevitable illusions.* New York, NY. John Wiley & Sons.

Pipher, M. (1996). *The Shelter of Each Other: Rebuilding Our Families.* New York, NY: Grosset/Putnam Book.

Poulin, C. (1998). *Nova Scotia Student Drug Use 1998: Technical Report.* Halifax, NS: Province of Nova Scotia

Prager, K. (1995). *The psychology of intimacy.* New York, NY. The Guilford Press

Quadrel, M.J., Fischoff, B. & Davis, W. (1993). Adolescent (In)Vulnerability." *American Psychologist, 48,* No. 2.

Rice, F.P. (1999). *The Adolescent: Development, Relationships, and Culture.* Toronto, ON. Allyn and Bacon.

Sebald, H. (1984). *Adolescence: A social psychological analysis,* 3rd ed. Englewood Cliffs, NJ: Prentice-Hall, Inc.

Seifert, K.L. & Hoffnung, R.J. (1994). *Child and adolescent development,* 3rd ed. Toronto, ON: Houghton Mifflin Company.

Selman, R.H. (1980). *The growth of interpersonal understanding: Development and clinical analysis.* New York, NY: Academic Press.

Siega-Riz, A.M. & Popkin, B. (1998). Three squares or mostly snacks: What do teens really eat? *Journal of Adolescent Health, 22,* 29-36.

Siegler, R.S. (1986). *Children's thinking.* Englewood Cliffs, NJ: Prentice-Hall.

Simon, R.W., Eder, D. & Evans, C. (1992). The development of feeling norms underlying romantic love among adolescent females. *Social Psychology Quarterly, 55(1),* 29-46.

Stevens, N. M. (1996). Rural Adolescent Drinking Behavior. *Adolescence, 31,* 159-166.

Sullivan, H.S. (1953). *The interpersonal theory of psychiatry.* New York, NY: W.W. Norton.

Vartainian, L.R., & Powlishta, K.K. (1996). A Longitudinal Examination of the Social-Cognitive Foundation of Adolescent Egocentrism. *Journal of Early Adolescence, 16,* 157-178.

Wadsworth, B.J. (1989). *Piaget's theory of cognitive and affective development.* New York, NY: Longman.

Webber, M. (1991). *Street kids.* Toronto, ON: University of Toronto Press.

Wexler, D.B. (1991). *The adolescent self.* New York, NY: W.W. Norton.

William T. Grant Foundation, Commission on Work, Family and Citizenship. (1988). *The forgotten half: Non-college youth in America.* Washington, D.C.

William T. Grant Foundation, Commission on Work, Family and Citizenship. (1988). *The forgotten half: Pathways to success for America's youth and young families.* Washington D.C.

Index

AGMV Marquis

MEMBER OF THE SCABRINI GROUP

Quebec, Canada
2000